THE PLACE WHERE SOULS ARE BORN

THE PLACE WHERE SOULS ARE · BORN ·

A JOURNEY TO THE SOUTHWEST

THOMAS KENEALLY

INTRODUCTION BY JAN MORRIS

Hodder & Stoughton

LONDON SYDNEY AUCKLAND

Sou
17/11/92

A CIP catalogue record for this book is available from the British Library

ISBN 0-340-57382-1
Copyright © 1992 by Serpentine Publishing Company Pty Ltd, 1992
Introduction Copyright © 1992 by Jan Morris
First published in Great Britain 1992

Published by Hodder and Stoughton,
a division of Hodder and Stoughton Ltd,
Mill Road, Dunton Green, Sevenoaks, Kent TN13 1YA.
Editorial Office: 47 Bedford Square, London WC1B 3DP

Printed by arrangement with Simon & Schuster Inc., New York

Manufactured in the United States of America

To my daughter Jane,
natural traveler and buoyant companion.

CONTENTS

INTRODUCTION
by Jan Morris

It is always fascinating to see how novelists, especially novelists of the first rank, handle their talents when it comes to the writing not of fiction, but of travel books. Sometimes they treat a journey as a plot, a place as a character, and the experience of travel as a surrogate for a love affair, a tragedy, or a self-exploration. Sometimes they obey with particular discipline what one might call the classic unities of travel narrative—starting at the beginning, recording a journey chronologically, ending at a destination. And sometimes, with the fling of the creative artist, they produce something that is really in a genre of its own, abiding by no conventions, perhaps because they feel that in pursuing this, the most flexible of literary forms, they are on artistic holiday.

Thomas Keneally, among the most variously brilliant of all contemporary novelists, is certainly no respecter of orthodoxies. One of his most famous books, *Schindler's List,* created a celebrated literary commotion when it won the Booker Prize in England in 1982, precisely because nobody was quite able to define it, and I think critics may find it equally difficult to pin down *The Place Where Souls Are Born*. It is an extraordinary mixture of descriptive writing, meditation, history, reportage, memoir, and philosophy, subtly attached to the presence of a landscape—the unforgettable landscape that extends southwards from the Colorado Rockies to the Mexican border of the United States. Countless novelists have been attracted by this stunning country, so alive is it with history and suggestion, with the fire of American innovation and the beauty of Indian tradition, and to more ordinary travel writers too it has been an inexhaustible source of purple passage.

Mr. Keneally illuminates it, though, from an altogether different perspective, because he is an Australian. He is a New Man in the southwest, bringing to its mountains, deserts, and pueblos comparisons born out of the Outback and the aboriginal encampment. He is full of surprises—for us as for himself. He is also inexhaustibly interested in things, and his enthusiasms seem to me curiously distinct from those of Europeans or Americans. Everything seems fresher and clearer seen through his eyes, whether it be the rituals of skiing, the origins of Mormonism, the Navajo cuisine, or the complexities of drug smuggling over the southern frontier.

Most magically of all, somehow or other Mr. Keneally gives to this record of a journey a suggestion of the universal, as though the terrain, the characters past and present, the tangled currents of history, the curiosities of observation and experience, the ever-present suggestion of vast skies, snows and sunshine, are brought together by the writer's alchemy into an apparently inevitable whole. Such is the chief purpose of the novel, and as this book shows, it can be the higher purpose of travel writing too.

•

PREFACE
Travel, Travel

WHEN JAN Morris, the famous travel writer, invited me to do a book like this, I suggested three possibilities. One was the Sudan. There is a great book to be written on that bitter, lovely republic. But I decided on grounds of logistical complication and danger too excessive for my present purpose and situation in life to leave the Sudan to someone who wants to make his legend and who is willing to take a notable risk to do so.

Australia was another passion, but Jan Morris and I decided that perhaps it was too obvious. Who can trust the impressions of a man who is writing about his own land? Well, it isn't an entirely conclusive argument, but it is a strong one.

As for the Southwest, I had been excited by it in the cinemas of my childhood but learned from my first journey into the area in the mid-1970s that I'd received only a narrow, partial and inaccurate segment of its story. I was taken by its difference—a physical difference, a different sort of space, the space of enormous elevations of mountains, of canyons deep enough to make the brain creep and waver.

•

Then there was the inveigling similarity. The similarity between Leadville, two miles high in the Rockies, and Australian mining towns, for example. A town like Leadville was fed from the same immigrant impulses and dreams which made the Australian frontier town. To visit the Leadville Catholic Church, a hushed environment in itself, doubly silent amidst the snow, is to step back into the church I knew as a child in Kempsey, New South Wales. The memorial windows are dedicated to the same kinds of people—Mr. and Mrs. Charles Murphy, Mrs. Ellen O'Brien, Mr. and Mrs. Patrick Quinn, Mr. Ernst Hofstadtler, refugee—like so many Colorado miners and Australian dairy farmers and miners—from Bismarck's *Kulturkampf*; or else a plain old Bavarian economic refugee.

Australian mining towns like Castlemaine in Victoria are full of nineteenth century hotels which, like the Clarendon in Leadville, have now seen the best of their traffic but which are sisters in the spacious mineral-boom architecture of the nineteenth century.

There is for me therefore a sense of being both at home and abroad in a town like Leadville. An Australian has to keep on referring to the snow and the heights to remind himself that this is not some town in western New South Wales. It is as if similar passions have run through the earth's crust and core and made an organic link between the two places.

WHEN I was a lad at a Catholic high school in the Western Suburbs of Sydney, some radical intellectuals in the class used to subscribe to the *Catholic*

Worker, Dorothy Day's left-wing and socially aware New York broadsheet. The editors were always reporting on some project or other they had going with the Hopi Indians in Arizona. I knew nothing about the Hopi, except that they were not amongst the catalog of tribes which usually gave trouble to Randolph Scott or John Wayne on Saturday afternoons. I knew nothing of their profound history, because American popular culture offered me not even a garbled version of it.

In the mid-1970s, camping through Colorado with my then young children and my wife, I received a fragment of America's ancient history of the kind which would ultimately surface in the Hopi of Arizona, and was transfixed and inflamed by it. I stood at an overlook in Mesa Verde National Park and saw, in a large cavity beneath the cliff across the canyon, the beautiful twelfth century Anasazi pueblo called Spruce Tree House. Who were the people who had lived in such well-ordered townships beneath the brows of the cliffs? This part of the world had once, while the Roman Empire still existed and then through the European Dark and Middle Ages, been populated by excellent people, people of artistic and social and technical resource. The Anasazi, the Hohokam, the Sinagua. Their descendants are the Hopi of Arizona, for whom Dorothy Day canvased resources, and the Pueblo of New Mexico.

I was so taken by the Anasazi that I considered writing a novel about them. It is fair to warn you that there will be a lot about them in this book. But if you can tolerate that, be sure that you and I between us are readjusting a curious imbalance. Every time I have been to the Southwest and then go on eastward, I talk passionately about Anasazi places like Mesa Verde, Canyon de

Chelly, Betatakin and find that few of the skiers of Vail or even citizens of Denver have been there. America's human antiquity does not evince much enthusiasm in Americans. It is as if it were essential to Americans' view of themselves to believe that nothing much went on in the Southwest until prophecy and greed descended on it in the 1850s.

So, since every book is based on an arrogant intention, since a belief that there is something readers should know is the only thing to sustain a writer, I wanted to produce a book which made the antiquity of the Southwest obvious and—again the arrogance!—engrossing for those who read it. A book which might change for good the calibrations of their minds whenever places like Arizona, Utah, New Mexico, or Colorado were mentioned.

REVIEWING A travel book of V.S. Naipaul's on the South, a *Village Voice* writer made the point that it's hard to write about a particular region in the developed world anymore. Even thirty years ago the way of life of the South was entirely separate from that of the North. But now the *lingua franca* of McDonald's and Sears and Midas Brake and Muffler facilely unite every corner to every other corner. So too the *lingua franca* of sitcoms made in California and soaps made in New York. All this, the reviewer said, reduces the particularity of any place in America.

And what does the writer do? Does he ignore these manifestations, the branches and franchises which employ and preoccupy so many of the locals? Does he limit himself to the fragment of exotic history kept in museums and a few historic buildings at the core of the town, the part where the people who work at Sears and Midas rarely visit and cannot afford to live? Does he concentrate on hunting down only the *remnants* of the particular, the regionally unique?

The dilemma faces someone writing about the Southwest. Even in Tuba City, on the Navajo reservation in northern Arizona, where until the 1960s there were merely the octagonal Tuba Trading Post and the Tuba City Truck Stop Cafe, there are now a Kentucky Fried Chicken, a McDonald's, an Arby's, a branch of Bridgestone tires. Citicard can be used at the Texaco gas station to withdraw money. Does the writer limit himself to Navajo rugs and jewelry and tales of the Navajo's depredations against the Spanish, the Mexicans and the Americans, and the depredations suffered in return?

There's a sense in which Citicard and all the rest of it are a challenge to the writer and a sense in which they are a stimulation. For in the Southwest, the strangenesses persist in the face of the tendency to make the known world one great mall. The Sudan is certainly easier to write about in that way. There are no Kentucky Frieds, and Mastercard is meaningless. Every regional group wears different face slashes or cicatrices, has a different song, a different dance, a different jewelry design, a different and conveniently visible living folklore. But there is still a side of the life in the Four Corners of the Southwest—and not only in the Hopi, the Navajo, the Zuni, the Pueblo, but even, for example, in the life of the Mormons—which goes totally untouched by Citicard and the mass emotions of television and commerce. There are impermeable centers of exotic civilization in the Southwest which remain strangely resistant to the reduction of all

•

of humanity to one, universally manipulable consumer. What astounds me is that America pays so little attention to these powerful pockets, is so underinformed about these features which deliver it from its impoverished urban dimensions.

ONE

Front Range
à la Vogue

THE VOGUE Cinema was an art deco picture theater on Parramatta Road, Homebush, a western suburb of Sydney in which I spent the second half of my childhood. None of the glamour Americans rightly see in Australia seemed attached to Homebush. The place was noted mainly for its abattoirs and for its biscuit factory which filled the suburb with a shortbread fragrance every Wednesday. The Vogue picture theater though was—as cinemas were everywhere—our place of dreams and our secular cathedral. No one in Homebush had a staircase which approached for amplitude and aquamarine carpet the sweep of the Vogue's staircase. The statuary, moldings, and stucco grandeur all came from the other side of the Pacific and were in the best, excessive, Californian tradition.

It was here and not at school that I first heard such names as *Rockies* and *Denver*. Or rather, it was here that the names had power and mythic meaning. When we moved down to Sydney from the bush, I went to the Vogue for the first time. It was with my digger (Australian soldier) father, home on his last leave before disappearing into World War II for two and a half years. I remember only one image from the outing. It was of a man in chaps, a gunbelt, and a big hat riding hell-for-leather across a table top mountain on a big black horse with a lariat at its withers. When the man-and-horse reached the edge of the flat-topped mountain—I didn't have the term *mesa* in my vocabulary—this wonderful cowboy machine went back on its haunches and slid down the escarpment, making plentiful dust.

Who was this magical man-beast and where was this magical landscape? I was sure it all existed only on emulsified film. That there was no place like that.

I went to the Vogue every Saturday until puberty temporarily gave me less primitive tastes. If I knew that the following Saturday there was to be a romantic comedy or a musical, I was desolate. I abominated Ginger Rogers and Esther Williams; they caused an almost physical revulsion. The discovery on a Monday morning that next Saturday's picture was to star Miss Williams poisoned the entire Homebush week. I longed for movies with Southwestern landscapes, though I still had no idea where on earth they were. The very look of the mesas and canyons and of ponderosa pines were a pledge of excitement. If I saw in the opening frames the megaliths of Monument Valley (of whose existence and location I was utterly ignorant) or likewise the great canyons of Sedona, I knew that that first infatuation with mesas and cowboys would be enriched, that I would be transported. The landscape of the Southwest never disappointed me.

•

THE PLACE WHERE SOULS ARE BORN

An opening frame of New York, by contrast, with some jaunty, fatuous music over it, promised nothing but boredom. I was a stupid and innocent child, and I was wrong. But only half wrong. I was right about the Southwest.

I cannot go to Denver and to the Rockies now without taking the mythology and the childlike expectancy with me. On my dreaming map, the Homebush Vogue and Denver—though in brute fact some eight thousand miles from each other—are more than next door neighbors. The one colors the other. Denver succeeds or fails, excites or disappoints in terms of what the Vogue led me to expect of it.

At the start of this journey, as on earlier ones in the area, I found it hard to absorb the size of Denver and its politer cosy suburbs. The Rockies rise above them like dreams. From Denver's office towers and hotel windows, you see the beginning of the Front Range, where most of the Vogue's great gold rushes started.

This is the terminus of the Great Plains, which run all the way from Appalachia to the lowland Colorado towns east of Denver. The proposition the name *Denver* still raises is that from here on America changes. And it was always so at the Vogue. The Cheyenne, Arapaho, and Kiowa gave way to the Ute. There were maps shown at the start of many a Western which told you such things. The map showed places the Ute or the Kiowa attacked catching fire one after another on the screen. How were Wayne or Scott to quench such fires?

For me, even the road map of the region is great reading and still has connections to those blazing and graphic maps I saw at the Vogue. On the plains there are towns which were named to honor vanished forts (Fort

•

5

Morgan), vanished hopes (Last Chance), vanished scouts (Kit Carson County), and vanished Indians (Wild Horse). Once the mountains begin, the towns and settlements are named for mountain springs and lakes and for cherished minerals. The Great Plains enthusiasm for philosophically planned and urbane farming settlements—Greeley, say—gives way to the raw chaotic mining town in some breakneck canyon—Cripple Creek.

The suburbs of Denver appease the past tragedies of the Great Plains and of the Rockies. With homely, orderly streets, they gloss over the desperation of seekers and travelers. In Denver for example, there's an extraordinary multistory bookshop as big as a department store, employing hundreds of staff in this era of shrinking literacy. Every renowned writer who goes on a promotion tour knows of this store and nominates it as perhaps the finest, the most comprehensive in America. As much as it is a delight, one wonders how trigger-thin Randolph Scott would have fitted it into his world scheme.

While Buffalo Bill is buried in the foothills to the west of the city, the name invoked in the city is not that of Bill Cody but that of the quarterback for the Denver Broncos, a team which boasts of the mile-high Denver air they breathe as if that requires a chosen act of daring.

The Rockies save this new Denver, light years in pretension from the threatened little settlement of the mid-nineteenth century, from its average urban dreariness, and yet seem remote from the town. You get the feeling that on many days, many of its citizens forget to lift up their eyes. The human traffic is heavy on this platform of foothills where the city stands. It takes your attention.

At Stapleton airport the question of whether planes

•

6

landing endlessly on parallel strips and on top of each other will survive preoccupies you. It took the former Vogue child and his wife and daughter some hours to rent their Montero four-wheel drive for their winter swing through the Southwest.

This should have been a splendid moment and, in a way, was so. The vehicle was to take us through the Four Corners, the North American region best loved in the Vogue and in later adult travels; a zone unified by deserts and mountains and a shared antiquity which make you think differently than you would anywhere else in America. But so many square miles of rental vehicle yards surround Stapleton that no sense of the particularity of our journey allayed the long bureaucracy of the rental. In the wait for the keys, it seemed longer ago than Mycenae since the vastly spread and aggrieved Ute caused Washington to consider abandoning Colorado to them. It seemed longer ago than the Nineteenth Dynasty of Egypt that the depletion of surface gold caused its population to leave by thousands and reduced it to a squalid, haunted cantonment.

Now it has its Performing Arts Center and its many-sided Art Museum where Renoir and Monet, Degas and Chagall share the space with the pacified and surviving art of the tribes. A good thing too. A triumphant thing. But I have been to the Jeu de Paume. In Denver I am a child wanting to be into the mountains. At the Vogue I did not go for Esther Williams; here in Denver I did not come for the Impressionists.

WESTWARD ACROSS the city, reckless with its spaces like many a city of the zone, like Salt Lake or Phoenix or Tucson or Albuquerque or other fat cities of the recent wilderness, the same Rockies that the Vogue presented do, however, sublimely lie. The grown child can't believe the luck of being permitted to drive toward them. Are they somehow diminished though? For the Denverites go near them not to pursue the mad dreams which were the Saturday afternoon cowboy norm. They go to divert themselves. To ski or—in summer—to ride bikes.

The road west is skirted by malls and discount mattress warehouses. Then just beyond the mattress and furniture barns, the mountains *really* start to assert their reality. The nineteenth century mountains. And the towns made and then left in the lurch by mining—all as at the Vogue. Hotels and public buildings built by mineral fervors hunch under the snow in canyon bottoms, often far below the level of the big highway west of Denver. They aren't far west of the city either, these towns which have always got the sun late and lost it early. Towns like Idaho Springs or Georgetown, above which the skiers fly along toward their chosen slope, pausing only for gas and cheeseburgers.

Turn that name on the tongue. Idaho Springs. The flavor of it.

It still looks raw. It is removed from the Denver of the airport and car rental by more than the literal distance. It is old Colorado and is unabashed about imitating old Colorado's squalor: a blend of motor homes and of flamboyant old civic structures, built by mineral patriarchs who, for all they knew, were building for a metropolis.

THE PLACE WHERE SOULS ARE BORN

Idaho Springs is the sort of town which still gives reality to the sort of day suffered in the 1859 account of a Missourian called George A. Jackson. As quoted in a modern road atlas of Colorado, in the one day Jackson had first to "build big fire on rimrock to thaw the gravel: kept at it all day." Then a wolverine came into his camp, was killed by his dogs after he was forced to break its back with a belt axe. "Hell of a fight." Such days still lie pooled in the dark bottom of Idaho Springs's canyon.

Then Georgetown. What a study, though the skiers fly by it.

A Frenchman called Louis Dupuy, former seminarian, journalist, and deserter in the Wyoming Territory from the Second Cavalry Regiment, built a hotel here which still stands, the Hotel de Paris. Its style again is—as it were—unrevised. No fresh flow of ski resort money has led to any tarting up along the lines of the rejuvenation of the old Hotel Jerome in plush Aspen. Yet the Hotel de Paris was counted very fancy in Colorado's seasons of ore. Healthy, mineral-laced glacier water was run by tap into all the rooms of the Paris! Hot water was also on tap! A fountain full of trout occupied the center of the restaurant!

At least two Presidents slept there, and rail and silver barons, and members of the Booth family of actors. But very few skiers descend from the freeway to see Dupuy's great hotel. They are bent for the slopes of Keystone, Breckenridge, Copper Mountain, Vail. They hope for powder snow. They hope to get in a maximum of runs before it turns icy about 4 P.M.

THE MOUNTAINS seem so pristine, yet—closer up— you find them part-shaved of trees and groomed to make runways for downhill skiers or to receive the ascending chairlifts. Skiing is the impassioned industry of the mountains now, in this landscape which seems to lunge from one questionable fury to the next. People speak of skiing with the surefire enthusiasm and the speculative fear which was reserved a century past for lead carbonate.

I had strapped to the rack of the four-wheel drive vehicle our cross-country skis, my daughter's downhill. I am myself a downhill skier though a poor one, so I do not ask so much with environmental piety as in wonder: Did ever a human diversion, a diversion for what you could call ordinary people too, require such an imperial infrastructure as this? Did the medieval boar hunt, preserve of the nobility, or did the jousts such as the Field of the Cloth of Gold, demand more labor, more energy of all kinds than the daily business of the Colorado snowfields along I-70? High-speed quad chairs or gondolas eke to heaven, hauling skiers in brilliant, windproof fabric up the mountains. The skiers, dangling their skied feet over groomed voids, talk to each other about where they come from and where they're staying and of their doubts whether they have the mettle for this slope. But the immensities of space absorb what they say, absorb the swish and sighs and clickings of the chair. Sometimes, for mechanical reasons or because someone has fallen getting off at the top, the chair stops above some near-vertical Black Diamond slope, and you sway, wondering in gaudy ski-clothes about the stories of underdressed skiers perishing of hypothermia before they can be released from broken-down chair lifts, as the wind comes chiseling across the face of steep snow.

•

THE PLACE WHERE SOULS ARE BORN

Skiing intoxicates people. It gives human beings a chance to be baroquely arrogant, in fact, and divinely brave. It gives them a chance to dress more flamboyantly than any male has been empowered to since the close of the Napoleonic era. Businessmen who would not be seen in anything but gray suits and burgundy ties on the New Haven line are allowed here to dress in fluorescent lime. Taboo is lifted. The stockbroking or accounting elder is permitted to put on windproof motley.

All along I-70 and elsewhere in the Rockies there is a system of peonage behind this glittering business; a class of young who are willing to take low wages and long hours for the chance of skiing frequently and for free. Cowboys, in effect. Cowgirls. For they seem nearly as short of a private life as those who brought cattle up the trail named for Jesse Chisholm. Nearly as stupified by the sameness of the long days, the ceaseless greasy creak and slap of the chair cables.

Some greet and discipline you on the ski lifts. Their name tags say, "Cathy Baker, Wilmington, Del" or even, "Denise Chapman, Melbourne, Australia." You may meet them moonlighting *après-ski* in the bars of Vail or Aspen or Breckenridge or Steamboat Springs. Aerobically refined young men or women who taught you to parallel ski that morning serve you your margarita at 5 P.M. They tell you they don't know if they can survive this way for life, but many of them aspire to. And the analogy to cowboys again: They seem to sign on readily for one more season.

They have in fact the same highly refined contentment, determination, and spirituality that you see in really good surfboard riders in Hawaii and Australia. Every day I am at home at Bilgola Beach outside Sydney, I see and

•

am fascinated by such excellence. The acolytes of snow have a similar, enviable, pragmatic contentment as the surfers. Do the sociologists of Boulder study them, I wonder?

There are unseen members of the subclass as well, the men who drive the grooming machines at whatever angle the mountain proposes. The machines are great, wide tractorlike contraptions with a cab located between their massive tracks. As you eat dinner in the valley, all you know of the drivers are the lights of their machines, working on precipices of snow and somehow not toppling. The drivers of ski-grooming equipment are generally husky, solitary men from all over the world.

I have sometimes met them in bars on their days off. They too satisfy the cowboy archetype. They drink ruminatively and speak in short, careful sentences. It is not that they don't particularly have much time for the people who use by day the slopes they prepare so dangerously at night. They don't seem to think about them much. The slope-grooming seems to be to them an abstract task, like mowing your own lawn.

Like the young of the ski lifts, they can't always afford to live in the ski boomtown itself. Their quarters are off on some state road, north or south of the main highway. There they might live in trailer parks, crowded in mobile homes, finding privacy when their roommates are rostered on shifts different from their own. The mainly young servants of the Vail slopes, for example, live in part in West Vail or in Minturn, a small railway town in a cramped valley on the way to Leadville.

Vail then is new Colorado, a developer's plush idea of a Swiss village where Cartier and Armani happen to have franchises. Minturn is old Colorado, where the sun finds you in your narrow side valley late, illuminates modest civic buildings and services: the general store, post office, and VFW post. Where some of the citizens, who describe themselves as "real people", still scrabble in the ironhard winter earth for molybdenum.

One morning in a snowstorm, I was riding a ski lift at Beaver Creek, going up to the beautiful bowl of snow called McCoy Park. McCoy was an old man who logged timber up there during World War I. Some of it ended in Flanders as duckboards for trenches, but that's another matter. Over the top of the downhill ski run which the lift to McCoy Park also services came eight snow-grooming machines in convoy, edging homeward, the panzers of the night, nearly chimera in the slanting snow.

What could they have thought of all night in their snow-blinded cabins? They had this continuity with Randolph Scott: their job was perfect for men with pasts and long, reticent, and wistful memories.

McCOY, THE high bowl in the mountains. I had been there in the past, along with my wife, who was there this time too. Aerobics at high and lovely altitudes have a very humanizing influence on a marriage. We had recently learned to be passable Nordic, or cross-country, skiers, and although we were on our way to the antiquities and literal mysteries of the Four Corners region which were to be the meat of this journal, we believed conscientiously the account would not be harmed by a day or two in McCoy Park.

A Coloradan would not know what a strange plea-

•

sure the Rockies give an Australian—even apart from anything to do with the myths of the Vogue. I came from a dry and relatively flat continent, despite its immense size (about the same in area as the continental U.S.) low in elevation. It boasts the world's oldest river and many of the world's oldest and most worn-down mountains. The summit of its tallest mountain is barely higher than the village at Vail.

By contrast, beaches, in which Australia is profligate, never seemed novel to me. Certainly not in Florida or Southern California. Australia does beaches better, more sweetly, less perilously or poisonously than just about anywhere in the United States.

But I never saw snow until I was twenty-nine and flew to McMurdo Sound in Antarctica. Our aircraft landed on the frozen, eight-feet-deep ice of the sound, and I got down upon the dry, dry sea ice and went ashore, Antarctica's great desert of snow crackling beneath my space boots. I thought: This is the most remarkable form of precipitation, and it should be pursued.

Such was my awe for the stuff, I did not learn to ski until I was in my late forties. I took to Nordic skiing with a ham-fisted zeal. For it was the transcendental and zen-ish form of skiing. It was always a trek and a pilgrimage. It demanded no fussy technology to get you into position (McCoy is an exception in that way), and it brought you to an uncrowded splendor.

I will talk somewhat, in passing, about the experience of skiing into ancient sites in the Southwest, and I ask you not to find it offensive or hubristic if I say that should you be hale and enjoy minimal courage, there is no reason you should not do likewise. For you will be exalted in ways I find hard to articulate.

•

THE PLACE WHERE SOULS ARE BORN

McCOY PARK lies in a bowl of snow near on eleven thousand feet up. The ski lift to it passes over the Beaver Creek home of former President Gerald R. Ford, a muscular man, a former football player and zealous downhill skier.

The trails around the park—a word whose Southwest meaning we'll look at later—are groomed by a far more modest machine than those which work the downhill slopes. I am more at home with this plain technology than with the massive works of Vail and Aspen. This Nordic machine does however run two tracks, two indentations, broad only as the width of a Nordic ski. Up here you can travel along them for thirty miles, if you have thirty miles a day in you. You can climb hills, herringboning up the steep ones. You can slide down them at whatever speed you like, governing it all, including turns, by putting weight on this ski or the other. Your boots are light and are not fixed at the heels. They bear no resemblance to the massive boots downhill skiers have to use to protect their legs and ankles. Dare I say, they leave you more human?

In my night reading in the Rockies, I was diverted by the tale of an astounding nineteenth century ski.

It was undertaken by a Missourian called James H. Crawford, who arrived in Colorado in 1872. By the middle of the decade he was running cattle at Hot Sulphur Springs up in the north of Colorado. Now he went off to the west to reconnoiter pastures near Steamboat Springs, eighty miles away from his home, through the threateningly named Muddy Pass. He liked the wide expanses of the Yampa Valley pastures he saw, which the traveler to Steamboat still sees with elation from the top of Rabbit Ears Pass.

During the winter back in Hot Sulphur Springs, brooding in a cabin with his wife and children, he became anxious that someone else might preempt him. He put on skis hewn of wooden planks and made off through the late winter snows, across bitter country, *ungroomed* country. He wanted to build his cabin on the Steamboat Springs and lay other signs of human occupancy before the snows melted in the spring.

Of course, *human* occupancy there already was—the Ute Indians. It has become in part unfashionable to honor even such modest imperialistic thrusts as that of Mr. Crawford on his plank skis with their leather bindings. But nonetheless, anyone who has ever tried something as steep as Muddy Pass, testing enough even for a motorist let alone a Nordic skier—and not immune from avalanches either—would feel a little awe for Crawford and the exhaustion inherent in his journey. To fall late in the day in that deep powder would have exacted a terrible effort to get up again.

You would think that in the glittering resort at Steamboat, a chair lift could be named for him. He who thought himself a mere cattleman, but who was as well a form of American champion.

A S YOU work your way down from McCoy Park to the bottom of the mountain, happily following the road old man McCoy sent his logs down during World War I, an unalloyed glide, you come across the so-called

THE PLACE WHERE SOULS ARE BORN

Trapper's Hut sitting on a knoll at the edge of the descent to Beaver Creek. From here there is sublime prospect of the central valley of northern Colorado and of the Rockies. Descending to the *soi-disant* hut with you is a crowd of spectacularly accoutred young Japanese or Brazilians, some of them carrying video cameras in one hand so that they can tape their girlfriends rolling along beside them at twenty or thirty miles an hour.

To invoke Randolph Scott once more: he—the Randolph of our Saturday afternoons—would be really lost in this Trapper's Hut. It maintains its own French chef, its own wine cellar, its own backcountry guide. Whenever people set out to ski from this hut, they travel with a guide cum instructor and a further red-and-blue suited young man on a snowmobile who tows a stretcher and a sophisticated medical kit behind him. Such is the headiness of staying at $800 per couple per night at the Trapper's Hut that the skiers from it move seignorially about the mountain. It grows hard to work out whether the stretcher is for the young Japanese and South Americans or for others whom they might topple in their glory-struck passage. This is to live like Henri IV, all on a computer executive's salary.

But there *are* people in these mountains with whom Randolph and James H. Crawford would feel kinship. There are the backcountry tourers who go out for days at a time wearing steel-edged skis; descending mountains which have never seen a grooming machine and making that graceful, gravity-negating turn named telemark after a region of Norway.

The mountains are full of lean, brave men and women who can trek and Nordic ski race and snowshoe. They eschew the aggressive conviviality of the downhill

•

slopes. Outside Aspen, at a place called Hunter Creek one day a few years past, my wife and I enrolled by accident in a survival Nordic skiing course which we mistook for a normal excursion. We traveled up a superb valley marked by the huts of nineteenth century miners and by abandoned farmhouses with their second-floor doorways for when the first floor was snowed under. Here we met a solitary snowshoer, bareheaded, lithe, glowing with sweat, sinking in the powder to his thighs, his dog wading in the furrows he made. He was what they call "an aerobic animal." He was in training for some snowshoeing expedition to Nepal.

The Rockies are peppered with these aerobic animals. At Beaver Creek in January, they hold a triathlon race for the species. The first leg is the ascent to McCoy Park using skis, not the chair lift. The terrain is so steep and sometimes so icy that the competitors have to stick "skins," which look like strips of carpet or fur, to the bottoms of their skis for adhesion to the mountainside. Once up the precipice, they race round McCoy Park with the skins off before clamping on telemark skis for the precipitous descent to Beaver Creek and finish with a snowshoe segment of ten miles.

There is no external glamour to this sort of skiing. Training all the lonely year for such an event doesn't provide the skier with the audience which a good downhiller has every time he steps off the top of the chair lift. Sometimes the Nordic athletes will train in lonely pairs, lean husband and lean wife. Such contentment is not always seen on the downhill slopes. The Nordics are outright skiers in that they ski purely for themselves.

I use my own skis merely to make a self-paced way through country too absolute in grandeur to be called

•

merely pleasant. It is my hope, for example, even as I spin around McCoy Park, ultimately to encounter Anasazi ghosts that way on the mesa-tops in Colorado's far corner.

I have done some back country skiing in Australia, in the Snowy Mountains, which are less precipitous than the Rockies and not given at all to avalanche. The back country slopes in the Rockies are highly given to it. You see its signs everywhere—the treeless shutes down which avalanches habitually tear.

Even a contemplative and unaggressive skier can encounter avalanche. Rabbit Ears Pass, above Steamboat Springs and named after a nearby triple summit shaped like rabbit ears, is exquisite country but given on the right day to slippages. From the pass road you ski some three-and-a-half miles north—it is very beautiful—and emerge from trees and see before you a notorious slope. If temperamentally you resemble me, you do not test its bareness, even if someone valiant in the party suggests that it's okay to cross it one at a time. You turn back into the trees and have a happy, more or less downhill glide back to the road.

Storms of either kind can trigger avalanches, I read with fascination in the warming hut literature. Cold snaps which cause one layer of snow to fracture from the others. Warm snaps which can lubricate an upper layer of snow and make it easy for it to roll. Wind can do it too. Slopes facing north usually avalanche in dry conditions. Slopes facing south are a danger during warm periods and springtime. "Wet, spring avalanches," say the helpful notes, "are very heavy and quickly kill people who are caught in them."

There are instructions even for the unspeakable happenstance. If you're caught, "use swimming motions to stay on top of the snow. This is much simpler to do in a dry, light avalanche, than in a wet, heavy one. When you finally stop . . . put your hands over your face and push the snow away. The object is to get some airspace. There is plenty of oxygen in soft snow and you can survive a burial in such snow a very long time. Most avalanche victims choke on the snow . . .

"Now for the most difficult task of all if you become buried—remain calm! This takes a lot of concentration but is your only hope."

FROM TRAPPER'S Hut near the top of McCoy Park, above Beaver Creek in Colorado, you may look down into the high valley where lie the condos and bars of Vail. Behind you and further south are those of Aspen. Over to the east lie the other two great ski industries called Breckenridge and Copper Mountain. Off to the northeast are the peaks of the Lord Gore Range, which place a prodigious barrier between this great valley and that of the Yampa, where the cattle town and ski resort of Steamboat Springs is situated.

When I look down and out at all this splendor I do not so much think of crazy Lord Gore, though he's worth thinking of. Banging away at all the wildlife, he spent three years in this region in the early 1840s, accompanied by mountain men and by Ute Indians, whose jobs included the hauling of his enamel bathtub with the Gore family crest on it and the transportation from camp to camp of his wine cellar.

What I think of rather is that all this sublime coun-

•

try, and vast areas southward which cannot be seen from McCoy Park, used to belong to the Ute Indians. It is almost delicious to me to use such terms. Ute territory. It looks as it did in the better, Technicolor Westerns of my infancy. Like any of Saturday's children, enraptured in the dark and sucking on an Aussie concoction called the Scorched Peanut Bar, I knew the persnickety Ute would be driven off in the end. The prospect seemed a light one. But now I see what a loss of inheritance it must have been.

Ute country ran from the Front Range of Colorado over the Continental Divide and as far as the Great Salt Basin in Utah. It ran southward into northern New Mexico and maintained a turbulent, informal border with the Najavo in northern Arizona.

In the movies, the Ute always descended like thunder and in great bands. But like the Australian aborigines, they traditionally moved not in the masses of extras, whose thunder and war paint gave a frisson of upholstery-clutching terror to the Saturday afternoon young. They spent most of their lives in family groups, coalescing into larger groups for big ceremonies. A massed attack against, say, John Wayne's wagon train was not their normal mode. Nor were the actions which kept Denver under siege in the 1860s. All that was in fact their last, brave gasp.

It was—according to the orthodox belief—family group by family group that they took possession of their country in the first four or five centuries of this millenium. The last of them arrived—again according to the orthodoxy not everyone believes in—not long before the Spaniards. They were hunter-gatherers on foot until they got horses from the Spanish and became hunter-gatherers and raiders on horseback. Always, as now, they called

·

themselves *Nünt'z,* "The People." It is a name you still see on Indian cooperatives in southern Colorado, around Cortez, for example, and in eastern Utah, the areas they have been displaced to.

Ute is one of those Spanish-American mispronunciations or nicknames. The Spaniards called the *Dine'é* the Navajo because they saw them farming blue corn in little irrigated fields, and *Navajo* was the Spanish version of a Pueblo Indian word meaning "cultivated fields." Similarly the Apache—what heavy childhood magic attaches to that name!—carry the Spanish-American bastardization of a Zuni Pueblo word meaning "enemy."

The Ute—like the Apache and Comanche—have been declared reprehensible in the standard histories of the West, which say that they used to raid down into New Mexico, capture Pueblo Indians, and sell them into slavery to the Spanish. The idea is that latecomers, the Ute amongst them, preyed so fiercely on the settled Pueblo that the Americans were doing everyone a favor in suppressing the savages and sanitizing the frontier. It is only lately that some historians claim that the way the Ute behaved after the Yankees arrived to crowd them out was not necessarily the way they behaved before that great and traumatic apparition.

We remember from the Saturday afternoon pictures the phrase *Paramount Chief.* The Ute got their Paramount Chief, Ouray, merely because the Americans wanted one Ute leader to negotiate with. It was poor Ouray who had to preside over the breaking up of the Ute lebensraum. You see his picture in most town museums in the west and southwest of Colorado. He is frequently sitting with a railroad baron like David Moffat. First the U.S. government talked the Ute into receding

•

behind the Continental Divide. Everything between there and the far west would be theirs. But when minerals were discovered beyond the Continental Divide in 1873, the Ute were moved on again—to the extreme northwest of Colorado and into Utah or else to the extreme, arid southwest of Colorado and along a strip south of the New Mexico border.

KIT CARSON was an Indian campaigner from Taos, New Mexico; perhaps the only illiterate general who served in the United States Army but a remarkable man just the same. He forced the Ute's neighbors, the Navajo, into a concentration camp at Bosque Redondo in New Mexico in 1863. Long before that date, the Navajo themselves had learned to farm from the Hopi of Arizona.

But to the Ute, farming—the American Jeffersonian ideal—was always a heresy, an abomination, and an unwarranted departure.

The Ute were intransigent nomads and hence evoked two contradictory impulses in sedentary people like us—to condemn or to sentimentalize. They were dangerous fellows, a peril to European livestock and to European stock. Like the Celts, they honored warriorhood. They were stubborn. Despite the whole bitter history, the Ute Mountain Ute in their reservation at Towaoc (far away from Beaver Creek, down in the extreme southwest corner of Colorado) still won't farm, even though they consented long ago to graze livestock.

A SKIING instructor in Aspen told my daughter that a Ute medicine man had held a press conference at which he had cursed Aspen. That caused some primal nervousness in town, for the snow had been bad for some years. Others found it all too easy—in view of recent chancy seasons—to believe in the greenhouse effect. Others yet, as February still showed rocks bare of snow on Aspen's superb mountains, argued that it was all the heat which Aspen's opulent houses gave off into the atmosphere. It kept the snow up in the beautiful valley of Ashcroft and away from elegant Aspen.

It is not surprising though that the Northern, Southern, and Ute Mountain Ute accept the curse story. Later in the journey, when I got down to that region, I met a senior Ute in Towaoc, a member of the tribal council, a man called Norman Lopez. I mentioned tentatively that there must be some bitterness over the loss of the Ute country. He agreed but without rancor. "We still have medicine up in those mountains. Even if we don't ski there."

I T WAS probably a month after I was at Beaver Creek thinking of the Ute, after circuitous travel and many towns, that I met Norman Lopez of the Ute Mountain Ute, who live down in the southwest corner of Colorado, near Cortez and Durango, nearly in New Mexico, nearly in Utah. The literature says they have always been the most "traditional" of all. They were also reputedly the most observant of ritual.

I was on the Towaoc reservation too early to witness even in preparation the spring bear dance. The bear dance is a central rite of passage the Ute got from the Plains Indians and then adapted. The people on a reservation occasionally suggest, with an extraordinary pride, you should stick around for it. It is apparently an affair of enormous world-sustaining moment.

The sun dance they got from the Plains Indians is equally solemn and frequently mentioned—a mid-summer ceremony. Like a lot of tribal ceremonial, it demands a long, sober, and joyous preparation time. Lopez told me most kids know where the bear dance occurs and the locale under Ute Mountain where the sun dance is performed. Anyone who discloses the place or the details is exiled. Lopez used a very precise, faintly legalistic phrase, as if Ute terms had been translated into paralegal English: "Mental and physical disowning" was the phrase.

The most famous Ute Mountain chieftains—Buckskin Charley and Jack House, the latter of whom led the Ute Mountain people into the post-World War II world—are quite renowned traditionalists throughout the Ute community everywhere. The Southern Ute, who live over in La Plata and Archuleta Counties, northeast and east of Towaoc, have gone in for cash crops, as well as livestock. They are more "progress-minded," to use another commonly heard Ute Mountain term. In the Ute Mountain area, that term doesn't have any complimentary connotation.

Both groups are one though in that they run bingo halls by the side of the road to bring in revenue. The Ute Mountain Ute also own a construction company and a pottery works. But—again—no farm.

Since more traditional ceremonial life is so demanding in terms of time and intellectual effort, the Ute Mountain people have often run into trouble with the

•

educational authorities in nearby Cortez, where the children attend high school. Maybe because of this ritual stubbornness—which to European Americans looks like bloody-mindedness—they have suffered as scandalously as any group. It wasn't until the 1970s that running water was installed in Towaoc. Everyone over thirty can remember the times when water was brought in drums on the back of a truck from Cortez.

But even running water is an ideological business. Norman Lopez said, "I suppose water will make us farmers."

THESE UTE Mountain Ute have been engaged since the end of World War II in border disputes with the Najavo to the south, and so far the judgments have gone against them. They have lost precious mineral and gas royalties. A congressional bill to compensate them for these lost revenues was vetoed by President Jimmy Carter in 1980.

Wherever you travel on Indian land in the Southwest, you hear about border disputes between tribes. The problem between the Ute and the Navajo derived—like many of the others—from two contradictory government surveys. Boundaries were often incorrectly surveyed in the nineteenth century. The boundaries between the Hopi reservation and the Navajo in northern Arizona, for example, have also generated litigation.

Cultural differences figure highly in the disputes. The Hopi have been there for what could in practical terms be called a millenium. The Hopi town of Old Oraibi on Third Mesa is the oldest permanently occupied community in North America and is nearly as old as Dublin. Naturally the Hopi have a predisposition to look upon the Najavo and the Ute as interlopers.

I HAD met Norman Lopez in the circular headquarters of the tribal council beneath Ute Mountain. He is too genial a man to speak dramatically about dispossession. His chief renown, the renown which led him to election to the council, seemed to be a reputation as a storyteller. He appeared, too, to be of a further subgroup, the "progressive party" amongst the conservative Ute Mountain Ute. For example, the Ute Mountain reservation is full of superb Anasazi ruins reputed to be even more impressive than those in Mesa Verde National Park. Norman Lopez would welcome funds to stabilize them and open them to tourism. But the old people wouldn't like it, because, he said, the Anasazi still talked to them. There was a fear that the dialogue between the Anasazi and the older Ute will cease once the sites are opened wide.

During my afternoon in Towaoc with Norman Lopez, he studiously refused to express any bitterness over the great Ute dispossession. He compared the loss of earth to the death of an important man or woman. For, like Australian aborigines, the Ute do not mention the names of the dead or call up their images, for fear that the disconsolate and confused spirits, unable to take a clear direction home to their souls' source, will infect the living. He claimed that the lost country is like that. If you call up its name and dwell on it, it will make you sick.

Just the same, at Towaoc, there did appear to be plenty of anger and all the old problems of people whose mysteries are under threat. I gave a lift into Cortez to three Ute Indians, two handsome, secretive men and a very pretty, communicative woman. The woman was the most forthright and claimed to be the granddaughter of Jack House. She began telling highly circumstantial stories about the late chief in an attempt to prove it.

The three of them wanted to be dropped on the edge of town at a comfortless liquor store-cum-bar. The eloquent woman went in ahead of the others to check up if the store had a quantity of liquor appropriate to oblivion. "Sometimes the delivery hasn't come in," one of the men waiting in the vehicle softly explained. When she found the store was flush, she came out and got the others. The traditionalist doctrines of Jack Horse hadn't availed his putative granddaughter very much against the Yankee scorpion of drink.

Over in Utah, the Uintah Ute, who were driven out of northern Colorado, farm in the alluvial bottoms of canyons. Norman Lopez was worried at the idea that the Ute Mountain Ute might themselves need to begin farming in like fashion soon. To save them from even worse things.

TWO

Leadville Productions

AIL NEVER had a history as a mining town; it has no old railway depots, dives, and bordellos to restore. It has no ruined, leaning, unpainted cabins with the sort of fretwork under the eaves which miners and their wives favored in Minturn and Leadville and Silverton. Vail lacks Rocky Mountain melancholy. It is immaculate. No one goes hungry. The past does not scream. If minerals were Colorado's first boom and skiing its second, then the men and women who stroll amongst the bars and boutiques seem happy to be here, at this particular ore face, and to have missed the first one.

But there was never a western town like this in any of the dream palaces from Detroit to Manchester, from Dakar to Tasmania, where we picked up our iconography of the West.

Leadville is the antithesis of Vail. Like Georgetown,

•

it was made and then made old by minerals. It is wistful now, with its diminished population and with the gravity of its own quite estimable legends. This *is* a town from the rich darkness of all those afternoons before television brought us its cheaper and less pungent versions of the past.

Even the passes you have to go through to get to Leadville from the north are cinematically worthy. On one of them, on a spur which drops down perpendicularly to the Eagle River, is an entire empty township called Gilman. The road exit to it is barred off and festooned with threats of prosecution for trespassing. Houses for two hundred people lie on the bluff under roofs enormously weighted with snow. There is no light in any window, no men going on or coming off shift, no women talking in the streets. The histories of families who lived here from 1915 until the mine closing in 1975 call mutely from the dark windows.

The town has been for sale for some years, and recently someone bought it, perhaps to make it a resort. Gilman's location on its spur is worth a thirteen-part serial. Never were there such prime locations for the runaway coach sequence, for the vertigo of the cliff-top fight; never such verticalities for heroines to cling to and miscreants to fall down wailing in self-pity and thwarted malice.

And Gilman is a great lesson in the ambiguity of mining, since in 1975, the year of the closing, gold increased to over $800 an ounce.

The tailings of the Eagle mine, named after the deep-cutting river far below Gilman, are spread down one flank of the spur the town sits on. A great fall of spoil as near-vertical as the canyon itself. There is gold worth some $60 million still in there, and perhaps $40 million worth of silver.

A FTER YOU creep down from Gilman's awful heights, there lies on the road south to Leadville a stretch of high prairie named Camp Hale. It looks desolate amongst its mountains and under its snow clouds. Tennessee Pass, another vertiginous experience, rises to the south.

Hale is a place favored by Nordic skiers, and the Tenth Mountain Division were trained there during World War II. I hadn't known the first time I went there that a camp for German prisoners of war was located there too, remote and—one would think—secure.

This time I read in my roadside atlas a diverting Camp Hale tale of fatuous zeal and adventure. A Harvard honors graduate called Dale Maple, a member of an engineering unit stationed here in the mountains and an enthusiast for the National Socialist ideal, sneaked during one of his leaves into the POW camp and posed for some days as a member of the Afrika Corps.

While in the prison camp, seeking out hardliners and taking ideological seminars with them, he made arrangements to help two German officers escape. This was in 1944, and you would think that by then the war news would have dampened Maple's zeal as a frankly declared fascist. But proving that honors graduates are capable of as much egregious folly as any of us, he bought a used car, malingered to get another leave pass, which he used to spend more time in the German camp, and then es-

•

caped with his comrades, transporting them toward Mexico. The three of them were arrested by Mexican officials just over the border.

It was a return to fairly routine captivity for the Germans, but Maple was sentenced to death for treason. Only after appeal and argument was he saved the firing squad and the sentence reduced to ten years hard labor.

This is all material—Gilman's travails and dangers, wicked and traitorous Dale Maple—which I would have savored at the Vogue. This would have been suitable anti-Esther and anti-Ginger material. Following the Rocky Mountains social realism and family drama of the tale of Gilman and the Eagle mine, Maple could be Leadville Productions number-two movie. We could provide him with a decent patriotic miner's daughter, at first enchanted by his palaver, from whose eyes the scales fall. She and the hero would chase Dale to Mexico, all the way blessing each other and American democracy.

BUT THE chief production of Leadville Productions is Leadville itself. At midwinter it sits low-slung at ten thousand feet, looking west to the Continental Divide and yearning—such is the scope of its decline—for the modest boom inherent in the next trout season. It is still concerned with at least one mineral, molybdenum, which is mined north of the town in the Fremont Pass, in the area exotically named Climax by the nineteenth century miners; a name which says something of the mineralogical frenzy of the late nineteenth century.

Climax, you are likely to be told in any coffee shop or in the one bookshop on Main Street, is the *biggest* molybdenum mine in the world, and it keeps Leadville alive, though not enough to justify the gloss paint which characterizes Aspen.

The elderly woman who generally shows people around the Tabor Opera House in the main street of Leadville is getting frail, and it is hard to find it open in winter. Leadville can't afford the fuel bill to warm the place. Yet some of the most notable men and women of America attended plays here, in this bijou theater, and the finest traveling companies in the world performed here.

The opera house's history is absolutely mainstream Colorado history. Mr. Horace Tabor went through all the Colorado changes and had President Ulysses Grant for a houseguest and President Chester Arthur for a witness to his wedding. He was a senator, a recidivist pauper, a postmaster, a magnate, and a partner to the supreme Rocky Mountain tango, the one he danced with Baby Doe. But his shrunken town cannot really afford his memory.

And though Vail can maintain its ski museum, Leadville can't open the Mining Hall of Fame on the hill by the Healy mansion later than three in the afternoon in winter. Basically for lack of traffic, and for the same reasons that keep the door of the Tabor Opera House shut.

At midwinter, when we went there, taking our skis with us for a little excursion around Camp Hale or the flanks of Tennessee Pass, the town of Leadville was anguished one way or another by a documentary just screened on public television claiming that runoff from the Climax mine was toxic. The lovers of wilderness, and the backcountry trekkers, skiers, and snowshoers who have found haven and cheap housing in Leadville, ap-

•

proved of the documentary. Augusta Tabor, Leadville's spiritual mother, who always saw the mountains as mountains, as divine declarations rather than ore bodies, might have agreed with them. But the spiritual descendents of her husband, of the renowned and exotic Horace Tabor, considered the documentary pettifogging and an insult to the integrity of Climax.

Except within his own marriage, Horace Tabor did not generally have to deal with environmental puritanism of the kind which had found expression in the documentary.

LEADVILLE MIGHT be a tedious name. It hangs heavily on the tongue and on the brain. Yet it was a town of Byzantine excesses, imperial exaltations, godlike rises, murderous declines. And Horace Tabor and Baby Doe are quite genuinely the Abelard and Heloise of the Rockies.

But that's anticipating the story somewhat.

Here is the screen treatment, suitable for Vogue viewing: Horace Tabor and his first wife, Augusta, come to Colorado from Maine. Augusta is solid and righteous and stable. Horace has tastes for flamboyance and liquor, though a dirt-scraping existence has given him little latitude. A stonecutter, he settled in Kansas, farming, but has given it up to rush to Colorado at the end of the 1850s. The Tabors work Golden, the town where Coors beer is now made. Then they go on to Cash Creek.

In 1860 Abe Lee, a Virginian who has been to California, finds gold in what will first be called California Gulch and will then be called Oro City and finally Leadville. His aphorism for the experience is reported in all the newspapers, especially Horace Greeley's. He looked into his wash pan and yelled, "I've got the whole state of California in this goddamn pan!"

When Horace arrives in California Gulch/Oro City/Leadville-to-be, dutiful Augusta is with him. On a frontier, whether it be Colorado or Australia, there are only two kinds of women, the tart or the immaculate mother, the "damned whores," as a friend of mine once wrote, "or God's police." Augusta is at the Madonna/God's police end of the perceived pole. Miners entrust gold and cash to her protection, knowing that even the lowest of humans will not touch her. Augusta is Leadville's first bank—the myth will have it that the repository is her blouse. Sensibly she soon has a safe shipped in. She will never want for the rest of her life, except when it comes to what could be called the wants of the heart.

Horace is a fairly hapless prospector, and so Augusta steers toward founding a store and a boarding house. Horace Tabor, postmaster as well as storekeeper, makes a policy of grubstaking the miners of California Gulch and Buckskin Joe.

In the darkness of the Vogue in Homebush, New South Wales, I never quite knew what grubstake meant. It was one of those movie words that had the redolence both of cunning and last chance about it. It was a stratagem of which Horace Tabor became the leading exponent in all the ore-bearing region—providing prospectors with groceries in return for a share of their findings.

To continue: In 1874 some black, volcanic rock is taken out of a gold claim on the hill behind Oro City and is assayed in St. Louis as lead carbonate rich in silver. Since silver was the standard of U.S. currency, lead car-

•

bonate becomes overnight the craze, and Leadville becomes the chosen destination.

Two German shoemakers, whom Horace Tabor has grubstaked, find lead carbonate in a mine called the Little Pittsburg. From his outlay of a few eatables and pick handles, Horace (and indirectly Augusta) will earn $20 million.

Source for the next scene: Irving Stone, *Men to Match My Mountains*. A man named Chicken Bill, who has been working a claim on Friar Hill on the edges of Leadville, takes a load of lead carbonate from the Little Pittsburg, two-thirds of which Horace Tabor by now owns, and puts it in his own mine. Through this deception, he is able to sell his claim to Horace for $1,000. Horace keeps his men digging at the site in any case and realizes within weeks a return of $500,000 on his lost $1,000. Because there *is* silver there. Everywhere Horace strikes a rock, lead carbonate manifests itself. The gods have breathed on him hard. He is the Silver King.

Tabor goes into partnership with the railroad baron David Moffat, another member of the Rocky Mountains pantheon. Travelers still encounter his name in connection with railroads cut along the sides of improbable canyons or arrogantly slung over terrible mountain passes.

Next Horace turns theatrical and builds the Tabor Opera House without sparing expense on its fittings or stage machinery, and when Moffat's Denver and Rio Grande reaches Leadville, bringing with it former president Grant, Horace entertains the former Union generalissimo both at the opera house and at many sparkling dinners at the Clarendon Hotel across the road.

In the midst of Horace's profligate wealth, Augusta stays calm, will not wear jewelry, patches her old clothes.

•

Horace decks out the Leadville fire department with red uniforms bearing his name and is elected lieutenant governor of Colorado. He buys a mansion in Denver. But Augusta is wary about that too. She will not exult with Horace.

One day in Leadville, while he is dining with his business manager, Horace sees a waitress who, in those nonanorexic days, is considered an exquisitely chunky pocket Venus. Her name is Elizabeth Doe.

Leadville has already known adventurous waitresses. The unsinkable Molly Brown got her start and her inside information waitressing in the greasy spoons of Leadville and will grow in personal wealth till she can afford a suite on the *Titanic*.

The malicious whisper to Horace that Baby Doe, a young Irish-Catholic divorcée from Wisconsin, has outlaid her last money on clothes and has come to Leadville specifically to entrap Horace. If it is true, then she will— Horace believes—show herself to be far more than a mere good time girl or a facile temptress.

Horace begins by installing her in a suite at the Clarendon Hotel, which is connected to the Tabor Opera House by an overhead enclosed walkway. His heart brimming, Horace crosses often from his office in the opera house into Baby Doe's plush ambience. Here is a woman of a nonpenitential cast of mind!

In the years since, this *via amoris* Horace took must have become insecure and been knocked down, because it isn't there anymore. Leadville Productions would need to reinstall it for the scenes where the righteous and the envious, often the same folk, point up at it.

Horace has by now built an enormous Tabor Opera House in Denver itself and is a partner in the spectacular

•

Windsor Hotel, where Baby Doe stays on her visits to Denver. He himself runs the state senate with boozy meetings at the Broadwell House. People tell stories about his crassness, such as that he had ordered the Austrian painter who did the curtain for the opera house to paint out Shakespeare on the grounds that he'd never done anything for Denver and to put in Tabor's own portrait instead. But these tales are muttered only in the corner of rooms. He is too powerful to be mocked face to face. He has a hold over the Republican nomination for the U.S. Senate.

He divorces Augusta, leaving her the mansion, and marries Baby Doe in St. Louis. He is in his sixties but a mere boy in his love, and he has found a girl who will accept jewelry and high fashion and rococo excess.

A frequent guest of his homes in Leadville and Denver is William Jennings Bryan, the only man ever to stand for the presidency without success four times running. Bryan warns the silver miners that the United States government is under pressure to convert their currency to the gold standard and that this pressure comes from England and France as well as from Eastern gold speculators. Up in another silver town, Park City, Utah, on the balcony of a former Union Pacific railroad depot (nowdays an Austrian restaurant), Bryan has exalted a crowd with the cry, "Let us not crucify man on a cross of gold!"

But it is hard when you are living a life like Horaces's, one of the most satrapal lives ever lived in the West, to listen to this sort of warning with any sort of reality.

And Horace becomes a Colorado senator! Even if the Republicans only allow him a thirty-day interim period in the Senate in Washington, he spends in that time

•

$300,000 on egregious entertaining. A portion of the money goes to his wedding feast, for he is able to delude a Catholic priest into marrying Baby Doe and himself in Washington in front of a crowd of guests, including President Chester Arthur.

But his infallibility in business and in the management of other humans leaves him all at once. When the miners strike, he orders in the light cavalry he has founded himself to suppress them. He is no longer Leadville's beloved man.

It is significant that William Jennings Bryan, the great defender of the silver standard, should suggest to Horace Tabor and Baby Doe that they christen their daughter Silver Dollar. The talismanic name doesn't work. In the Depression of 1893, a depression which leaves six hundred Southwestern banks broke, President Cleveland calls a special session of Congress and urges that it pass legislation to put the U.S. on the gold standard. The new law which results means that the U.S. government is no longer a buyer of silver.

There is within days no further market for it. This *demonetization* means Horace is worthless. The mansion goes, the opera house in Leadville and the grand opera house in Denver: all of it quickly too. Horace is, as they say now, heavily leveraged. The fall is fast.

People are delighted to predict that Baby Doe will vanish along with all these assets. But the wonderful thing for Leadville Productions is that she stays by Horace, sells her jewelry, goes into a small rented house with him. Irving Stone tells how she takes some of Silver Dollar's gold-leaf birthday albums, gifts from former friends, tears off the gilt lettering with which the child's name is inlaid on the cover, compacts it into a small lump of gold,

•

and sells it to a dealer. (What a prime scene this one is, if backed by a effective andante passage of the musical score!)

An old Republican friend arranges for Horace to be appointed postmaster at Leadville. He becomes a conscientious postmaster. Then—towards the end of the century, when Baby Doe is still young—they make a journey to Denver, a sentimental pilgrimage to his various former properties, and Horace begins to feel a savage pain in his side. It fells him. It is peritonitis. On his death bed, he instructs Baby Doe "to never let the Matchless [mine] go, Baby. It will make millions again when silver comes back."

Baby and her two daughters go back obediently to Leadville a few years after Horace's death and live in an abandoned tool house by the mouth of the Matchless. After the girls go off to their own grievous destinies in cities back east, Baby stays there waiting for silver to come back. In 1935 she is found frozen to death, her arms spread wide in the posture of acceptance she might have learned from her friends, the nuns at the Leadville convent.

Final credits roll.

IN THEIR legends, the Rockies are as rich as any of Saturday's former children were ever led to expect. Tabor is certainly still there, in the air of disappointment and thwartedness which hangs over Leadville. It is wonderful to be in Leadville on a cold, still winter's afternoon, ten thousand feet up in the Rockies, and to see how exactly, hand in glove, the Doe–Tabor phantoms fit the town.

•

THREE

The Last Place Butch Stayed

T IS hard to believe that when in the 1860s the Union Pacific decided *not* to lay its transcontinental track through Denver, predictions flew that the city would wither on the vine. Cheyenne in Wyoming, through which the railway *would* travel, following pretty well the same route as forerunners like Jedediah Smith and the Mormons, was meant to become the West's big city.

Such was the power of the rail. That power is still legible in today's Colorado. The truth was that railway barons often had reasons of barely licit profit to take railways in the directions they took them.

G ENERAL WILLIAM Jackson Palmer, who was driving the Denver and Rio Grande Railroad south from Denver, could have taken it through the former Colorado

•

45

Territory capital of Colorado City. But that would have meant buying ground for depot and railroad hotel at town prices. Instead he decided to take it some miles east, over foothills acquired cheaply by his land acquisition subsidiary. The spacious, in fact enormous, town of Colorado Springs, which was in this way generated by the railway, became in quick time the county seat, the state's second largest city. It is home of the U.S. Air Force Academy, gateway to Cripple Creek and Pike's Peak and Ute Pass and to that Garden of the Gods which General Palmer used as a landscape incentive to court the girl he loved back east. "Could one live in constant view of these grand mountains," wrote the man who had killed Colorado City, "without being elevated by them into a lofty plane of thought and purpose."

The railroad, wherever you see it in these mountains, was more than a steel track. It reinvented the map for the sake of real-estate profit. Sometimes it competed with other lines to be the first to reach somewhere where silver had been found. It was the late nineteenth century version of the toll road, and it drove over passes previously accessible only to mules, and then it laid down its charges. It generated the map we have. It canceled with the heaviest hand ever the map that was.

But occasionally, particularly in Colorado, geography was too much for it. One of the reasons Denver failed to attract the first transcontinental railroad was the height of the passes to the west of the city.

One of the Rocky Mountain passes the pro-Denver lobbyists touted in Washington as a possibility was Berthoud Pass, amidst precipices about forty miles west of the city. In our rented four-wheel drive we made the enchanting but terrifying passage over it one brilliant win-

ter morning. Berthoud gets its name from a military sur-
veyor who breached it in 1861. Like most European
discoveries, the pass had been shown to trappers by the
Ute earlier in the century. The Ute had been using it for
some four hundred years.

The pass is eleven and a half thousand feet up. At
that height, unless you have lived in the area for months,
your breathing occasionally stops for one heartbeat, and
even sitting still you find yourself gasping every dozen
breaths. There are brochures available on that too: altitude sickness, dissuading you from taking backcountry
treks until your system is used to the height. The brochures tell awful stories of embolism and coma.

Like Rabbit Ears Pass, Berthoud is prone to avalanches. Great snowmasses pend above the traveler. Mile-
long cornices spike the sky and wait for gravity to per-
suade them down. It is not only because of altitude problems that Berthoud is what I would call *traumatically*
high. The trauma that country like this is most likely to
impose is a psychic one.

I found myself frequently confessing to my wife and
daughter that certain places in the Southwest produce in
me a kind of immensity phobia. The heights and spaces
are so massive a person can feel the suspicion that some
insupportable enormity, an advance on the one you're
actually facing, is just around the next curve.

An organizer of rafting expeditions down the Colorado and through the Grand Canyon told me that the
only two instances in which people had signed on for the
journey down the Colorado and through the Grand Canyon and then, at the water's edge, had a crisis of confidence had been due to this space phobia. A lawyer from
New York—admittedly the very person Westerners would

like to see suffer such a shock—hunched on one of the Colorado sandbars under the escarpments, blinkered his eyes with his hands and said, "I can't stand the size."

I know that feeling, though it hasn't yet stopped me. In the Canyonlands of southeast Utah—over which Butch Cassidy escaped after raiding the bank in Telluride, Colorado; in which the Mormon polygamists hid from a bitter federal search in the late nineteenth century—I felt threatened by the scale of things and grew secretly but piteously grateful to take refuge again inside a vehicle. I wonder how brave Butch looked it in the face all day, traveling on horseback.

It is a credit to the chutzpah of railroaders that David Moffat, Horace Tabor's former partner in a number of silver mines, wanted to put a railroad through Berthoud Pass. I applaud the cheek of the man too. First, even to my intimidated eye, it's obvious Berthoud Pass spectacularly contravened the 1862 Pacific Railroad Act, which ordained that the transcontinental railroad should not have grades greater than two percent. There was also the reasonable question about who would dig the trains out after the avalanches came down on the line. And finally, a railroad would require a three and a half mile tunnel through the Berthoud Pass granite.

The envisaged railway wasn't built in Moffat's lifetime. Berthoud Pass remained a wagon route for the gloriously named Central Overland California and Pike's Peak Express Company.

The railroad tunnel named for Moffat was at last driven through the rock in 1927. It received limited use. It is now used for other purposes. The Denver Water Board rents the Moffat tunnel to transport water from the Pacific side of the Rockies to the city.

•

BEYOND BERTHOUD Pass you are in a country
where the nineteenth century lasted much longer than
anywhere else in the West. The last living children of the
pioneers up there in northwestern Colorado are still in
the old folks' homes. Geographic features here haven't
had their American names for long. The ranch and village
of Tabernash, for example, is named for a Ute Indian
shot down by a posse from Hot Sulphur Springs because
he would not abandon his traditional ground along the
flats of the Fraser River. (The Northern Ute asserted their
sense of property by then killing a homesteader.) One of
David Moffat's engineers named the town after the fallen
Tabernash when the Denver, Northwestern and Pacific
Railroad reached the area a considerable time after the
company's establishment by Moffat in 1903.

In the same vein of relative recentness, the name
Meeker, on the White River, resounds for the Northern
Ute. This name—I remember from the childhood dark—
was invoked by both Errol Flynn and Robert Taylor as a
pretext for heroism. The aura of martyrdom attached to
it.

Here is how Meeker's name achieved currency in the
Vogue and came to be attached to a town in northwest
Colorado: Nathan C. Meeker was a former agricultural
editor of Horace Greeley's *New York Tribune.* He was a
passionate temperance man and led a group of readers
of the *Tribune* to eastern Colorado to found a temperance
colony called Union. When he grew tired of the complaints of the other temperance settlers, he applied for
the job as federal agent to the Northern Ute. Naturally,

he hoped to whip them into the same state of sober industry he had failed to impose on the Union colony.

Meeker hoped to discipline the Ute by withholding food and restricting their movements. When there was a reaction, he sent to Fort Fred Steele in Wyoming territory for U.S. soldiers.

Two hundred cavalry men descended on the Indian agency and camped by a mountain which has since been named after their commander, Major Thomas Thornburgh. Influential Ute began to ride up and tell Thornburgh not to move. They seem to have known that they would not be able to control their constituents if U.S. troops entered the reservation.

Thornburgh continued, however, and the Ute reacted by massacring Meeker and eight other men on the agency and taking his sixty-year-old wife and his daughter hostage.

Hundreds of Ute kept Thornburgh's men away and virtually beseiged them for a week. Thornburgh himself had been killed in an early countercharge. But his troops were at last reinforced by some fifty black soldiers. (They had been on patrol to the east because of the murders of Tabernash and the white settler.) The final lifting of the encirclement came when a relief force of eight hundred and fifty cavalrymen rode up.

Ultimately Mrs. Meeker and her daughter were released, and the Ute lost the whole of northwestern Colorado for what happened to Thornburgh and to Meeker. President Rutherford Hayes signed the Ute Removal Act in 1880, and the eviction took place in the years thereafter. But no one believed it would all necessarily work, and settlers were exercised till the beginning of this century by fears of a Ute breakout. The last time the Ute crossed

•

the Green River at Jensen's Ferry Utah, trying to ride back into Colorado to demonstrate their discontent, was 1903.

Today as you drive through Fort Duchesne or Roosevelt or Myton, Utah, on the way to Salt Lake City by the less direct route, you see the face of the evicted Ute. It looks up at you from the swings and jungle gyms in the schoolyards, from beneath baseball caps and out of the windows of trucks. It is a face which has come a great distance. From their supposed (though now challenged) nomadic Asian origins, across the Bering Strait, and southward between the great North American mountains. *The Nünt'z.* The possessors of Colorado.

The Americans tried to turn them into farmers. As we have already seen from the Ute Mountain Ute, to nomads farming is more than distasteful. It is literally an heretical activity, since it separates the nomad from his world picture and the ritual necessities of his seasonal travels. Nonetheless, the Northern Ute certainly farm in the canyons of the Uintah and Ouray Reservation in Utah. You could say Meeker had won.

THE CHILDREN of the northwestern Colorado settlers, the ones who are still capable of reminiscence, remember the dispossessed Ute. In towns like Craig, for example. It wasn't until the end of the 1880s that the Reverend Bayard Craig, Protestant minister and land speculator, came up over the passes from Grand Junction and saw this country before returning to Denver to launch a pastoral land company. Grand Junction was itself a youngish town—founded 1882. How curious that

•

this stripling of a municipality in western Colorado should later, in 1962, be the proving ground for the shopping mall, that it should be the Bethlehem of the real estate developer.

The town of Craig itself is barely a hundred years old. It has seen in capsule everything one would expect of the West—Indian decline, summary justice, mineral booms, conflicts between cattlemen and sheep farmers. I went to the library in Craig to see if there were any elderly children of settlers I might be able to talk to. They said there was a woman called Leona (Babe) Rector Henricks, native of the area, born in 1905. She was too ill to talk to now, but she had left an account of her early life with the library. I sat down on the advice of the genial librarian on a steely morning in a remote town to read Babe's account.

Photographs of her from the 1920s show a clear-eyed handsome girl with a retroussé nose, long lips, and an accommodating smile. She stands by her horse, clutching a Winchester and wearing army pants and lace-up boots. Everyone's dream girl of the West, suitable to be sung to by Gene Autry, another of the Vogue's icons.

So here is Babe remembering the dispossessed Ute. "We always received presents at the time of a birth in the Jim Rector family. They [the Ute] would bring bead and moccasins and whatever. . . . one old Indian came to the ranch and wanted money to buy firewater. My mother was there alone, and she said, 'I have no money.' He said, 'Oh, Jim Rector's squaw got money.' He said, 'Bring it back two moons.' Of course, a moon is a week: that meant two weeks. Mother argued with him for quite a while, and he started to sing. He was going to sing for

•

52

the money. So finally to get him out of the house she gave him some money. . . .

"She [Mrs. Rector] would wake up some mornings, and the whole dining room would be full of Indians sitting on the floor. They'd come in so quietly that nobody would hear them. They were always very hungry. They could eat platters of steak and taters and biscuits for breakfast, and then they'd leave and go quietly on their way.

"The Indians appreciated what you did for them. A bunch of them were living down the river. They all, of course, traveled by horseback. In coming to Rangely one day, this squaw with a baby strapped in a papoose board on her back had her mare run away with her. The strap broke and the baby was thrown into the rocks and brush. They came on across to the old Brick Ranch with the baby to see if mom could do something for it. Mother did: She took care of it the best way she could, but the baby was severely injured and died a short time later."

THERE'S A word that dominates this part of Colorado and the northeast of Utah and which casts light on the late-surviving frontier in the region. The word is *park*. It doesn't mean what it means everywhere else. Every frontier casts up such words: Australia, for example, produced the name *squatter* for grandee holders of enormous stretches of pastureland, and *station* for ranch. To a nineteenth century Englishmen, *park* might have evoked rolling country and planned copses surrounding a fine British garden and a country home. To the more rough-hewn

•

53

Americans it meant anywhere in a canyon bottom where floods had dumped enough good soil to make farming or grazing a possibility.

Sometimes the name is capitalized, as in the case of Winter Park, an old cow town turned ski resort, where many of the young men are ski instructors by winter and cowboys in the summer. It is capitalized too in the case of the notorious Brown's Park, a beautiful but remote canyon in the extreme northwest of Colorado. This corner was the last hole for outlaws, who could easily jump the border into Wyoming. It is semiarid country, very eerie and impressive, full of snaky, flood-prone creeks and mesas composed of sedementary rock. Butch Cassidy presided over the seventy-five-member Wild Bunch here as late as 1897, after they had been pushed out of the Hole-In-The-Wall in Wyoming.

The son of devout Mormons, Butch exercised his alternative dark bishopric for the last time in Brown's Park. Three Brown's Park teenagers were inspired by Butch and his legion to raid the bank in Meeker in 1898, and were all shot down as they emerged from the building. Even so late in the century, the old frontier ritual of keeping the boys' corpses on display and photographing their dead and strangely seraphic faces in their coffins was followed. The pictures are there in Meeker's town museum.

PERHAPS THIS last flash of doomed Brown's Park lawlessness convinced Butch that he should seek other options. When the Spanish-American war began, he and the Wild Bunch proposed to ride into Steamboat Springs and offer themselves to the United States authorities as

•

a volunteer cavalry unit. The possibility that the law officers might wish to try rather than recruit them gave them pause.

Ultimately, as the world discovered from Paul Newman and Robert Redford, Butch would leave the parks of northwestern Colorado and choose Bolivia as his zone of operations, dying there with the Sundance Kid twelve years later in the same way his three acolytes had died in Meeker.

Through infamous Brown's Park, the word *park* took on a meaning additional to that of (often poor) bottomland: It acquired a redolence of hole, hideout, illicit sanctuary.

The capitalized word has a somewhat odious connotation in Utah, too, through notorious Park City, a Gentile (non-Mormon) hot-bed in the mountains above Salt Lake. It chiefly carried in the Southwest a less spacious connotation than it did everywhere else in the world: a connotation that had nothing to do with space but more with skimpiness and poverty, with the tenuous and the melancholy.

In what is now Dinosaur National Monument in eastern Utah, a Brown's Park widow named Josie Morris lived from 1914 until 1964 in a modest park created by the floods in Cub Creek. We drove into what had been her home on a grim winter's day with snow threatening.

Her nephew helped her to build the cabin during World War I, where she lived fifty years on the border of Utah and Colorado, all without vehicles and electricity. One of the benefits of Josie's kind of park are the box canyons which run down from the mountains and can be used as *de facto* corrals for cattle. Some of the rails she used to corral her livestock remain.

•

Josie was alone in her Cub Creek park the day her horse knocked her flat and fatally broke her thigh.

By that stage, military advisers were already in Vietnam and President Kennedy had died. So if you had to nominate someone as the last nineteenth century woman of the West, the solitary Josie Morris might qualify.

It is—by the way—in similar narrow parks that the Ute in the Uintah and Ouray Reservation do their farming.

ON THE border of northwestern Colorado and Utah, between Vernal, Utah, and Craig, Colorado, and not far from notorious Brown's Park, the northernmost traces of the wonderful canyon-dwelling, village-making American heroes—the Anasazi—can be seen inside the Dinosaur National Monument.

Even these northerly, pre-Anasazi remains are eloquent. Again, we visited them in winter, in dry, biting cold, with no other vehicles around, and they produced in the three of us, late in a pessimistic century, an inveigling pride in the human species.

Along the canyons of Dinosaur, snow picked out the layers of rock, settling on the more durable sandstone, which I think is called Navajo, and leaving the more steeply-cut Chinle layers bare. Americans who did not know they were Americans lived here in these canyons cut by the river, since perhaps as long ago as 1500 B.C. In the same season as the Declaration of Independence was signed, the Spanish Franciscan Escalente would call this old, energetic river by its European name: *Verde*, Green. The branch of the Anasazi who lived here are called Fremont by archaeologists, though they are generally considered part of the Anasazi. They began farming corn in the parks and living in settled townships; *pueblos*, as the Spaniards would later have it.

Here, just as everywhere else in the world, the shift to farming brought greater time for permanent works of what we call culture. At Mantle's Cave, these people left an exquisite headdress of ermine and woodpecker feathers. The dry climate of the canyons took care of it until its modern discovery in 1940. The Fremont left more quotidian objects as well—well-sewn moccasins and large fishhooks of bone and wood. Their storage pits for grain are here, with the husks of sustenance still in them. On canyon walls, they made paintings and outlines of their hands. Of these, the fine American writer Wallace Stegner, a Mormon and a conservationist, writes, "Most wistful and most human of all—the painted hand prints and foot prints, the personal tracks, that said, and still say: 'I am.' "

It is my opinion, however, based on absolutely unofficial, nonuniversity-funded experience of Central Australian aborigines, that ancient peoples never paint for the callow purpose of declaring: "I am." They paint as a means of maintaining the physics of the earth. They paint, that is, to produce those magical and astounding bounties—rain and the resultant animal and plant species—which we attribute to the laws of chemistry and physics.

Apart from the paintings, there are what the archeologists call *petroglyphs*. Australian cattlemen, who have inherited similar aboriginal markings in the case of their cattle stations, call them *rock-peckings*.

One of the finest paintings on the cliffs of Dinosaur is of the hunchbacked flute player. Far south of Utah,

·

around Sedona, Arizona, you also find him depicted in the canyons of the Sinagua. The Hopi Gray and Blue Flute Societies are responsible for enacting the Flute Ceremony every second year in mid August. They celebrate the emergence of the Hopi people and their flautist from the Third World, the previous ruined Hopi world. The flautist is a divinity who has had a long currency, perhaps longer even than Yahweh's. In some places he is called Kokopeli.

The later Ute, themselves, left a few rock markings here, and so did the eccentric loner Pat Lynch, who, like Josie Morris, did some solitary ranching here early in the century. Good old Pat pecked a sailing vessel right into the middle of a panel of Anasazi hieroglyphs.

THERE IS a little cave not far from Dinosaur National Monument headquarters which, for reasons of appalling cuteness, archeologists who excavated it one summer in the 1950s named the Swelter Shelter. There are a great number of pictures and petroglyphs here, notably of whirling suns and robust lizards, and a large, short-legged, broad-shouldered figure, another hero, an ancestor who apparently doesn't need long legs to pervade the earth. He too recurs further south, but this is his northernmost apparition.

The people who did their serious painting and pecking in the Swelter Shelter and made a superb figure of Kokopeli, close to human-sized, on the cliffs above Cub Creek, were of the basket-making Anasazi. They had not yet learned to pot. They left here in 800 for reasons known to themselves, ritual or climatic reasons, abandoning the place perhaps because it seemed to them now to be cursed with epidemics. Or perhaps they were driven away by the first-arriving Ute or Navajo, those frequently invoked bad influences of the Southwest. Though why the Ute and Navajo, in those horseless years, should have been quite the terror they later were is not explained by those who blithely cite them in connection with the departure of the Dinosaur people.

The history of the Anasazi and other pre-Columbians all over the canyon lands of Utah, Arizona, Colorado, and New Mexico is one of unexplained departures. In the San Francisco Peaks area of Arizona, one major group would be forced to move by volcanic explosions around Sunset Crater, and then having settled farther east on the fertile volcanic fallout, would move again ninety years later because of drought. To the Anasazi, as is apparent with the Hopi now and always, disasters were not mere chances of nature but symptoms of a disordered region. If a region cannot be restored by dances, rites, incantations, and enactments, then it becomes an irreparably failed world, and the group must find another, more viable version of the planet. The Hopi believe they are now in the Fourth and last version of a viable world and that this is their and our final chance.

Here then, along the desolate Green, beneath the northernmost delineation of the flautist, the northernmost trace of a people who have captivated this parched Australian imagination, I remembered once more that the Anasazi were the first factor I thought of when I uttered the word *Southwest* to Jan Morris.

•

FOUR

The Dinosaur and the Prophet

HE DINOSAURS lie where they fell at the portals of Utah. Or to be less dramatic, a flood in the Jurassic Age brought their bodies to a sandbar here, where scavengers ate the meat off their enormous bones.

These enormous beings, including the brontosaurus, for example, who combined the length of a sailing schooner with the height of an apartment building yet who carried a brain of only two ounces, were attacked while watering here by somewhat smaller, meaner, meat-eating dinosaurs and left their great femurs stuck in the sandbar. Although many of the bones are so oddly enormous, they have the look they have retained for 145 million years, the look of the recently slaughtered and casually felled animal.

Floods advanced and receded above the place of their deaths, the sandbar was covered. Turned to stone

•

along with all its animal remains, including—beside the dinosaurs—those of turtles and crocodiles and shellfish, this stone segment and all its fossilized dead tilted upward during the era of pressure in which the Rocky Mountains were formed. Hence the sandbar was converted to a near-vertical seam of precisely legible dinosaur remains.

Merle Douglass, collector for the Carnegie Museum in Pittsburgh, came here on the recommendation of cowboys in 1909. He followed certain geological clues, echoes of dinosaur-bearing country he had seen over in Colorado and Wyoming, and so on top of the hill he found his sidewise tilted cache of great skeletons. "At last on top of the ledge . . . I saw eight of the tailbones of a *Brontosaurus* in exact position. It was a beautiful sight." Douglass would dig into the layer and crate many dinosaur skeletons by wagon train to the railhead in Colorado for shipment to Pittsburgh. The remaining eloquent bones are still there, studding the rock face of a trench dug into Douglass's hill and now roofed over and provided with walkways by the Park Service.

Largely Brontosaurus and Stegosaurus, their rib cages and spines are everywhere, their bones sometimes savaged and scattered by mouths of unimaginable extent and ferocity, sometimes lying in perfect anatomical order. There is a nice resonance between the massiveness of the beasts and the massive, antique, canyon-riven landscape all around.

The Gentiles of Utah, of course, like to joke that it is not to be wondered that there are so many dinosaur traces in the northeast of Utah, along the trail the Saints took to the Great Salt Basin. In Utah, of course, a Gentile is not a non-Jew but a non-Mormon.

•

THE PLACE WHERE SOULS ARE BORN

One hears the standard one-line jokes and anti-Mormon quips in such centers of godlessness as Park City, a barely reformed silver-mining hell in the mountains above Brigham Young's line of march down Emigration Canyon into the Salt Lake Basin. In Park City, for example, I asked a woman in a bookshop if there was any work on how Gentiles achieved a portion of political power in the state. "Oh yeah?" she asked me. "What book would that be? It's got to happen before you can have a history of it!"

MY COPY of the Book of Mormon comes from a motel room in the berserkly divided desert town of Wendover, right on the Nevada border, on the further, western side of the Great Salt Basin. Wendover is a strange little border town, since halfway through it, Utah of the Mormons ends and Nevada of the unearned win and the slick-as-grease divorce begins. A large yellow line marks the place where this occurs, and one yard from theocratic Utah two towering neons of cowboys panning gold indicate that here is available everything the Mormon leader Brigham Young hated: speculation, greed, and the invocation of false gods.

The Utah side of the line is where you sleep if you wish to do so quietly or cheaply, though even there the Gentile motel owners run shuttle buses up the road to Nevada's scandalous Wendover.

The copy of the Book of Mormon which I possess is not the property of a Wendover motel owner but had been placed there by a man from Salt Lake City called Harold L. Davis. A sheet of paper with his photograph

•

had been inserted in the front of the book saying he wanted me or some other traveler to take it. In the photograph a genial, reliable-looking American face presented itself, lantern-jawed and—as Americans like to say—"together." Beneath the photograph there was a message. "The Book of Mormon is important to me because: it is a sacred record of God's dealings with the two great civilizations that inhabited the Americas."

The Book, recorded on gold plates which Joseph Smith dug up out of a hill called Cumorah near Palmyra, New York, on a September night in 1823 and which he translated with the help of two seer stones given to him by an angel called Moroni, purports to be the work of Moroni's father, Mormon. It recounts how the family of an Israelite prophet Lehi built a ship and emigrated to America about 600 B.C. The group ultimately split factionally and then racially into the Nephites and Lamanites. Centuries later, a resurrected Christ ultimately appeared amongst the Nephites in North America, living for a time amongst them and completing the fullness of revelations cut short by his death.

The Lamanites were—according to the Book of Mormon—the ancestors of the American Indians. The others, the Nephites, had suffered a decline, and about 421 B.C. vanished as a result of their spiritual divisiveness and folly. "And now," says Mormon to his son in the Book of Moroni, the last section of the Book of Mormon, "I dwell no longer upon this horrible scene. Behold, thou knowest the wickedness of this people . . . their wickedness doth exceed that of the Lamanites." Joseph Smith's task, according to Moroni, was to disseminate the book and call new Nephites to become Saints of the Latter Day.

•

THE PLACE WHERE SOULS ARE BORN

In the Wendover motel, on the quieter, Mormon side of things, I read Mormon's book for the first time. It is a remarkable document, owing much of its style to the King James Bible but showing a sense of drama and a good grasp of fable and parable.

At the head of the book stands the fascinating testimony of eight witnesses: "That Joseph Smith Jnr., the translator of this work, has shown unto us the plates of which have been spoken, which have the appearance of gold; and as many of the leaves as the said Smith has translated we did handle with our hands; and we also saw the engravings thereon, all of which have the appearance of ancient work, and of curious workmanship."

One of the eleven testifiers was Martin Harris, a New York farmer who would put up the money for the first edition of the Book of Mormon, and another is Oliver Cowdery, to whom Smith dictated from behind a curtain at his father-in-law's farm in Pennsylvania the translation of the gold plates. These testimonies are there because an early complaint of mockers and unbelievers was that the gold plates had never been sighted by independent witnesses. To which the Mormon answer was that if they had been, then faith would come far too easily. And in any case some of these early enthusiasts for Mormonism *had* seen them.

Questions to do with the validity of the testimony of those eleven early followers of Smith, and other questions of historic or devotional interest to Mormons, have generated sharp interest in early Mormon documents. When Martin Harris, the farmer and patron, asked to take 116 pages of an early translation home to show his wife, who had given him a lot of trouble over his support for Smith, the manuscript somehow disappeared. After that Smith

•

entrusted further translations to the perhaps less flighty Palmyra schoolmaster, Cowdery. But if that missing manuscript given to Harris ever did turn up, it would sell for the same price as a prime Monet.

IN SOME ways Mormonism is a genuinely American phenomenon. It grew straight out of the Christian fundamentalism which still influences America more than any other nation on earth. It could only have flourished too in a country where there was an immense, undesirable wilderness the just could clear out for and claim; an ordained oasis where the Latter Day Saints would live in safety and not be crowded out by other, more profane settlers. A prophet could not as credibly have led his people from London to Wales as he might from Missouri into the Utah nullity.

After Joseph Smith's death, then, the Saints did clear out under Brigham Young and travel to and claim such a massive quarantine area in the desert.

THE ASTOR Place subway station in Manhattan—in which the city's homeless huddle and shake their plastic cups, begging for quarters—is decorated with tiles depicting the beaver. John Jacob Astor's fortune was made in beaver trapping, and the first Europeans to penetrate the Rockies by way of South Pass, north of Utah in present Wyoming, were employees of Astor's.

It was thirteen years later, in 1824, that the famous American trapper Jedediah S. Smith made known to the world, particularly to his employers, General William Ashley and Major Andrew Henry, the existence of South Pass, a way up through the eastern elevation of the Rockies so gradual that wagons could mount to the pass at a pleasant crawl. Those trappers were the way they would later be depicted in celluloid: tight-lipped doers. The scout Jim Bridger, for example, who also followed the Bear River down to the Salt Lake and tasted its water and came to the belief that it was a wing of the Pacific. They were all working a long way from Astor's mansion in the square near the Bowery which bears his name, and when they found ways across the Rockies or discovered the Pacific in Utah, they suffered no impulse to announce the news in the *New York Times.*

Jedediah, who now has a chain of Utah restaurants named for him, was quite a literate frontiersman though, and he wrote of the area in terms which would be read with interest by the young, forceful Mormon Brigham Young. "I had traveled so much in the vicinity of the Salt Lake that it had become my home in the wilderness." It was Brigham for whom it would become home however.

In the days when news of Utah was first reaching the eastern states, Jedediah was involved in territorial trapping wars with the British brigade from the Hudson's Bay Company. The leader of the British group was Peter Skene Ogden, whose name is attached to a city north of Salt Lake. Ogden called Jedediah a "sly, cunning Yankee." He himself was, he said, "disgusted to find that Americans had already trapped nearly every stream along the Wasatch front."

The Wasatch Range and the Great Salt Lake belonged at that stage neither to Britain nor to the United states but to Mexico. Men like Jedediah and Jim Bridger,

·

doing the Manifest Destiny waltz without knowing they were, made it *de facto* American and unknowingly laid the basis for Brigham's coming Zion.

Those American settlers who traveled through Utah before the Mormons had a hard time of it. The first party was the Bartleson-Bidwell company, who were lucky enough to meet up with a group of mountain men led by Thomas Fitzpatrick. Legends, oh legends! The thirst, heat exhaustion, and miring of wagons and livestock in salty mud they experienced would convince most other parties to steer clear of Utah and take the longer, more northerly line westward. Influenced by Lansford W. Hastings, author of the best-selling *An Immigrant's Guide to Oregon and California*, who recommended the Great Salt Basin as a way west though he had never seen it himself, the notorious Donner party came down through Emigration Canyon, as Brigham and the others would soon do, and then were so delayed by the confusions of the terrain and the bogs of the Great Lake that, when hit by early snow at Donner Lake, forty-four of them would die of cold and starvation, and the forty-five survivors would be guilty of cannibalism.

Brigham's very different pioneer group of seventy-three wagons came down Emigration Canyon in the midsummer of 1847. For this entry into Canaan, Brigham was ill unto death from Rocky Mountain fever, the result of a tick bite. Yet even prone he gave the orders. One of his company, Erastus Snow, recalls him as saying: "This is the place whereon we'll plant our feet and where the Lord's people will dwell." A stone shaft in Pioneer Trail State Park at the eastern approaches of Salt Lake City is believed to mark the spot of Brigham's utterance.

At the end of the summer, when Brigham Young

returned to the Missouri Valley to fetch and succor other Mormons already on their way, there were already over two thousand Saints settled by the Great Salt Lake. It was while he was back in Council Bluffs, Missouri, that the Saints' ruling body, the Twelve Apostles, confirmed him as president, prophet, and revelator.

IF YOU wanted a landscape appropriate to prophecy and revelation, you could not do better than the site of Salt Lake City, with the sudden and enormous mountains behind and the rigorous nullity of the Great Salt Basin before.

Mormons still accept that the major force for wisdom on earth is the pillar of enlightenment from on high. The President of the Mormon Church, Ezra Taft Benson, President Eisenhower's Secretary of Agriculture and successor of the visionary Joseph Smith, is described by the Church of Latter Day Saints exactly as Brigham was: "Prophet, Seer, and Revelator."

So even as late as 1987, when the Church decided to ordain blacks to the two levels of Mormon priesthood—Aaron and Melchizedek—the late Mormon President Spencer W. Kimball and the two other members of his First Presidency announced the news not in any fashionable, civil rights argot or in terms of moral insight. The change was credited to revelation. "He has heard our prayers," said Mr. Kimball of the Deity, "and by revelation has confirmed that the long-promised day has come, when every faithful, worthy man in the Church may receive the Holy Priesthood." Mr. Kimball's statement of revelation included no reference to the extent

•

to which Washington's threat to count Utah out of certain federal programs might have hastened the divine voice.

America was never comfortable with the Mormons. In Smith's day, they were driven from New York to Kirtland, Ohio, to Independence, Missouri, and then back across the Mississippi to Nauvoo, Illinois, and from thence to the long migration into Utah.

The reasons conservative and even fundamentalist Americans have always mistrusted the Mormons seem to be complex. One reason must be that, despite the energy with which Mormons do business, Mormon life seems to encourage communistic and cooperative enterprise, and in America all that is far more heretical than it would be in any other country. Private enterprise America looked with some suspicion on Brigham Young's dying calls for equal profit-sharing amongst Mormons, and on the Mormon cooperatives in Utah: Brigham's Zion Mercantile Institution, the ZCMI, which claims to be the first department store on earth; the Cooperative Security Corporation; and the Deseret Mills and Elevators and Deseret Coal Mine Corporation, all of whose product goes straight to communal welfare.

The church's profit-making banks (Deseret National, Zion Savings), insurance, hotel, and sugar enterprises and the individual enterprise of such Mormons as the hotelier Marriott only partially reassure capitalist America. Utah's symbol—seen on fire and police vehicles and on highway signs—is the beehive, and to many Americans the beehive has been a suspect symbol: communism embodied in nature.

Principally though, the Mormon practice of plural marriage, abandoned under federal pressure in the late

•

nineteenth century but still alive in the 1990s, outraged national opinion.

The history of the connection between Mormon polygamy and the Constitution, Mormon polygamy and the United States, is an engrossing one.

VISITORS TO Salt Lake can rarely avoid discussing the polygamy conundrum both with fellow Gentile tourists to Temple Square and with Mormons themselves. For Protestant America, polygamy is the "but" in, "It's a remarkable organization but . . . ." To pluralist America, polygamy was the doctrinal fly-in-the-ointment for Mormons that papal infallibility was for Catholics.

Polygamy was one of the chief reasons the United States early tried and to an extent succeeded in breaking down the Mormon hegemony in Utah. The U.S. garrison commander from 1862, Patrick Edward Connor, encouraged his soldiers to prospect for minerals. He was the anti-Brigham. He tried to Gentile-ize Utah, to make it mainstream American, and was beginning by the mid-1870s to be excited by the progress of the place. He wrote, "The number of miners in the territory is steadily and rapidly increasing. With them and to supply their wants, merchants and traders are flocking into Salt Lake City, which, by its activity, increased the number of Gentile stores and workshops, and the appearance of its thronged and busy streets presents a most remarkable contrast to the Salt Lake of one year ago."

His troops found silver at what was to become Park City, the Gentile fleshpot and later ski resort in the mountains east of Salt Lake City. Connor succeeded so well that a numerous mining population of European Jews, Greeks, Italians, Scots, and Irish settled in Utah. But like most humans excited by a mineral boom, he believed that the tendency would be eternal, that the lodes would never run out, that silver prices would never fall, that monogamous Gentiles would never stop coming.

Another non-Mormon immigration would occur during the industrial boom of World War II and continues now because of the state's plentiful defense bases, proving grounds, and unspecified research centers screened by desolate hills. Even so the Gentile population is still less than a quarter of the people of the state. Gentiles still tell you frankly they feel more than outnumbered. They feel outmaneuvered and even outcast.

THE GENTILES seemed, too, for a long time to make little impact on the practice of plural marriage.

The Mormon historian, Leonard J. Arrington, implies that Joseph Smith would have read everything, even a growing affection for another woman not his wife, as a manifestation of divine will. "If Smith's religious sincerity is conceded, then he would naturally see the whole idea in religious terms . . ." Just the same, it would be fatuous to believe that all Mormons took up Smith's doctrine of polygamy with alacrity. When Brigham Young first heard of it from Smith, he claims, "It was the first time in my life that I desired the grave." When an orphan girl called Lucy Walker was approached by Smith and told that God wanted her to become his wife, she was horrified and prayed all night before "a heavenly influence" lit up her room and reconciled her to the arrangement.

•

In the days of plural marriage, while American opinion was engorged, titillated, and appalled by the practice, Mormons looked to the Constitution to guarantee their freedom of religion. Brigham, a pungent speaker, announced to the Saints: "There is not a single constitution of any State much less the constitution of the federal government, that hinders a man from having two wives; and I defy all the lawyers of the United State to prove the contrary. . . . I never entered into the order of plurality of wives to gratify passion. And were I now asked whether I desired and wanted another wife, my reply would be, it should be one by whom the Spirit will bring forth noble people."

When Brigham was indicted for adultery in 1872, he was forced by the federal authorities to travel in old age from the Mormon settlements in southern Utah, St. George and Dixie Mission, through snow-choked passes and the foothills of Wasatch to face trial in Salt Lake. In the midst of one of his court appearances on charges of adultery, the Supreme Court of the United States ruled that the criminal trials of one hundred and thirty-eight Mormon polygamists had violated the constitutional guarantees of due process.

So the Union and its courts would never reduce Brigham the way they have reduced lesser talents like the modern fundamentalist prophets Jim Bakker and Jimmy Swaggart. Brigham Young had prophetic and frontier endurance.

THE NINETEENTH-century clique of Utah Gentile mining magnates called the Utah Ring had business reasons for wanting the Mormons pursued to the limit of the law. Their lobbying and appeals to the federal sense of decency caused Congress to pass the Poland Act, and the pursuit of Mormon polygamists by federal marshals grew relentless. Sometimes marshals were led to polygamist hideaways by disgruntled first wives, but equally men were protected by first wives who rode through the night to warn the husband and the hidden-away second wife. The canyons of southeast Utah are studded with reference to the federal hunt for polygamists: Cohab Canyon, for example, which lies in the Moab area and of which one polygamist said, "A hell of a place to lose a cow, and a good one to lose a US marshal."

After Brigham's death, the federal government was induced to legislate to legitimize all the children of plural marriages up to 1883. But the hunt itself grew more intense, and the Mormons founded an underground railroad, like that which abolitionists had used prior to the Civil War, to hide and pass on threatened polygamists.

The disruption of farming and business, and even of normal society, became intolerable to bear. There was a political price too. The federal government legislated to disenfranchise polygamists, and a Gentile became mayor of Salt Lake City. It was when legislation was before Congress to deprive Mormons of U.S. citizenship that Mormon President Wilford Woodruff produced his manifesto against the practice of polygamy.

"Inasmuch as laws have been enacted by Congress forbidding plural marriages, which laws have been pronounced constitutional by the court of last resort, I hereby declare my intention to submit to these laws and to use my influence with the members of the Church over which I preside to have them do likewise." Other statements on the manifesto by Woodruff and senior

·

church leaders of the time would stress the revelatory aspects of the decision. "The Lord had ordered it and the Lord had discontinued it."

A suspicious U.S. President Harrison observed Utah for some time before returning confiscated church property, and it was his successor, President Cleveland, who authorized the admission of Utah to full statehood in 1896. Utah could elect its own officials without having unsympathetic federal ones foisted on it.

Now, nearly a hundred years later, the visitor is aware that plural marriage is still a vigorous institution in parts of Utah. In Ogden, to the north of Salt Lake, in St. George and Delta to the south, in Moab in the wild and desolate uranium country of the southeast, polygamy is practiced today by Mormon dissidents on the basis of Morman dogma as revealed through Joseph Smith.

Orthodox Mormons, who say that the time of polygamy is gone, nonetheless feel that "the blood-stained wicked nation" which pursued their forefathers so bitterly, supposedly for moral reasons but in fact for base ones, has now fallen on its own moral petard. A Mormon woman I met at the museum in Vernal, who had visited Australia to see her son on his mission there, a woman who was a partner in an obviously devout monogamous marriage, argued that in a way the polygamists had won the argument about the right to pursue their practice under the Constitution. There are, she said, so many Gentiles living in sin or in ménages-à-trois that all the sting has been taken out of the war on plural marriage.

Today the rustic and suburban polygamy practised in Utah does not project to the visitor any sort of seraglio splendor and glamour. For America's economy is based on serial marriage. So is the social welfare system and systems of inheritance. The days are gone when you can feed a host of wives and children, however eternally sealed, out of one harvest of wheat or honey. The American tract home is simply and obviously not built for polygamy.

We went driving with an orthodox Mormon of well-ordered domestic and commercial background in the prosperous town of Provo, home of Brigham Young University and of the disciplined, sword-of-the-Lord BYU football, basketball, and baseball teams. When polygamists' households were pointed to through the window, it was with the same timidity as a Gentile might show, with the same awe, shock, and whatever other emotions make up our reaction to plural marriage.

What you see of dwellings in polygamist enclaves in Ogden and Delta, St. George and Moab, is generally an unpainted and unkempt structure very much at odds with the traditions of Mormon neatness. There is no gloss of prosperity on the battered few vehicles parked in the drive. It is obvious that for the schismatic Saint and the Saint's wives and for their children polygamy is still a fierce calling, just as it used to be in the days when federal marshals pursued polygamist Saints with all the ferocity of America's majority ideology.

PLURAL MARRIAGE, while no longer countenanced by the clean-cut modern church, grew out of Smith's revelation that people could be "sealed" for eternity to their spouses and offspring, as well as to their own ancestors and even to other people's. Plural marriage would increase the number of children the faithful could beget

•

and through them give to the populations of dead spirits, howling in the darkness, a new life, a chance of being sealed forever to a family of Saints in this world and a succession of future ones.

This revelation about eternal sealing has visible form on the west side of Temple Square today, in the work of the church's genealogical division. Across the road from the temple and the famous tabernacle is the Mormons' main Family History Library. The *Guide to Research* which the library issues to those who go to look into their ancestry there sums up the theology thus: "Members of the Church also believe they can be eternally united with their deceased ancestors. They do this by making covenants on behalf of their ancestors, who can accept these covenants in the spirit world. In order to make covenants for their ancestors, members must first identify who their ancestors are."

A sign you see on the desks of library clerks says, "The Lord Almighty is planning a great family reunion, and we're lending a hand." For it is possible for a Gentile's ancestors, at the Gentile's request, to be "covenanted in" through what an elderly Mormon guide described to us—as exactly as the restrictions on disclosure permitted him—as "work in the Temple."

The library opened in 1894, but microfiche and databanks have given it a worldwide spread so that there are a great number of subsidiary libraries throughout the world. It is characteristic of that Brigham Young-style thoroughness of the Saints that they have twenty teams out in the field throughout the world, microfilming civil and church records. There is apparently some work being done now on African, Asian, and Arabic genealogy, but— in the pattern of Mormon, let alone American, race attitudes of the past—the libraries' records seem for the moment to be largely Caucasian.

It is just the same an astounding collection. The *International Genealogical Index* is on computer, so that on any day all the computers on the main floor are manned or womanned by those trying to bring their forebears up out of their immigrant obscurity. "The 1988 edition lists the names of over 121,000,000 deceased persons," says the *Guide to Research*. Given that the majority of these listings are—I guess—nineteenth century and that in 1900 there were only one billion people on earth, the Mormon compilers have done an extraordinary task of compilation, of garnering souls.

I wasn't able to find any of my name on the *IGI* nor in the family group records collection. But then the Keneallys settled either in Australia or in Brooklyn and seem to have had too much fear of their clan to desire to commune eternally with them. There were many of my mother's name though in the family records: Coyle, a Galway and Donegal name which many emigrants took from those stony northwestern Irish counties to the stony but more promising Southwest.

In the lower basement though, where you find civil, military, and criminal lists, church registers, shipping lists, census, probate, and immigration lists recorded on microfilm from sources throughout what you might call the *white* British Empire—Britain, Ireland, South Africa, New Zealand—I encountered some records of variously spelt Keneally settlers and convicts, including my great uncle John Keneally, Fenian organizer for County Cork and, in 1867, transported to Western Australia on the last convict ship of all, the *Hougoumont*. Likewise of my wife's great grandfather, Hugh Larkin, condemned to life

•

80

transportation to Australia in 1839 for a crime called "assault habitation." Mormon energy had confirmed family mythologies about vaguely remembered rebels, about the rural activist Hugh Larkin, about the great uncle whom the perfidious British had captured after one of John's coconspirators dropped the entire table of organization for the Fenian underground in Cork and Kerry out of his pocket while visiting a lavatory on a Cork railway station.

I suppose I could have pursued Uncle John to the upper basement, even if he hadn't made it into the *IGI* yet. For he died in the end in Los Angeles, and there was sure to be a microfiche version of that fact. I wondered had anyone "bonded in" John or Hugh Larkin or his convict spouse Mary Shields or any of the others and whether they lived rejoicing in one of the Mormon eternities, elevated from the bowel of penal ships to the eternal embrace of the Saints.

THE GENTILES and reprobates of Park City or Alta don't like you saying so, but there *is* a powerful authority to Salt Lake and its empire, even to the bulk of the church's public buildings in Temple Square, to the technological thoroughness of the genealogical library. You can argue about the validity of Joseph Smith's experiences back east, and it is hard in the demythologised late twentieth century to believe that Moroni led Joseph Smith to the gold plates with their "Revised Egyptian" script, dictated a translation to him behind a curtain in Pennsylvania, and then took them back for concealment again in the Hill Cumorah in Palmyra, New York.

•

But you cannot visit Salt Lake and feel the presence of Mormonism, its social, cultural, even its economic power, and not know that something astounding has generated all this.

This idea will suffer partial dilution when you see the efforts the church has gone to in the visitor's center, with its fairy-floss cloud murals and its coiffed Aryan Christ, to convince the rest of American Christendom that it is as devoted to Christ's primacy as they are.

Go across the road however and look at C.C.A. Christensen's naive paintings in the art gallery, and your sense of the potency and uniqueness of Mormonism will be restored. Christensen's works are American masterpieces, a sequence dealing with Mormonism's early wars and braveries, martyrdoms and immolations. You take from them a sense that whatever happened to Joseph Smith, farmhand and odd-job man, it was not mere shamanism, mere huckstering. An earlier prophet put it accurately: "By their fruits you shall know them." The tree of Mormonism does not bear fruit comfortable to behold, but it's hard to deny its yield is authoritative.

A S I intimated earlier, one of the fascinations of Salt Lake City is the number of historic documents dealerships you see in the business district. There is a feeling that even in the theocracy of Utah the faith is embattled, and that is simply one of the concepts which has begotten sharp interest in early Mormon documents and in what they show, one way or another, of early Mormonism.

Critics of the Mormon Church, such as Steven Naifeh and Gregory White Smith, authors of *The Mor-*

mon Murders, are amongst those who claim that documents embarrassing to Mormonism's public face, or harmful to faith, are secreted in a vault in the First Presidency Building in Temple Square. It is the sort of accusation which is easy to make and hard to deny. But certainly the First Presidency of the Church is in the market for documents, as the circumstances of the above-mentioned murders indicate.

The origins of Mormonism are arguably sullied by the folk religion and magic of the period and place Smith lived in and by overtones of "money digging," the use of divining to search for buried cash in western New York farms. In 1985 a Mormon document dealer named Mark Hoffman murdered two fellow Mormons with particularly savage homemade bombs and was himself injured when he made a mistake moving a third bomb out of the back of his car in Temple Square. One of his victims was the wife of a businessman involved in the authentication of early Mormon documents Hoffman had sold the Church of Latter Day Saints. The bomb was intended, of course, not for her but for her husband. The second bomb, which had detonated at the same time, killed a young businessman named Steven Christensen who, at the request of senior members of the church, had also been looking at the authenticity of some of the documents Hoffman had earlier sold the church.

The embarrassment to the church was not Hoffman's psychopathy but the fact that he had sold the most senior officials of the church a number of embarrassing and "non-faith-promoting" documents, all of them based on his substantial expertise in Mormon documents and history, yet all of them forged. One such forged document, supposedly signed by Joseph Smith himself, placed the

Mormon's succession in the hands not of Brigham Young, the lantern-jawed, tough, John Wayne-style prophet who would bring the Mormons into Utah in the end, but in those of Smith's son. There is still a Reformed Latter Day Saints Church in Missouri who believe in the son's succession, and Hoffman was able to get competition for the document going between both the officials in Temple Square and the leaders of the schismatic church.

It is significant of the way things stand in Utah, and of the way Utah stands to the Union, that Church leaders felt bound to buy these documents and hide them away. For they believed that they would be pilloried on any pretext, and their early history, and the history of their migration into the wilderness, and then what befell them in that wilderness, lends some weight to that paranoia.

Wallace Stegner, who was himself a Mormon, wrote of the embattled mentality of his brethren in what Utah Gentiles would consider accurate yet fairly flattering terms: "They stand facing the rest of the world like a herd of rather amiable musk oxen, horns out, in a protective ring, watchful but not belligerent—full of confidence but ready to be reasonable, and wanting to be liked."

MANY ORDINARY Mormons to whom one talks about this document fracas and other potential Mormon embarrassments speak with common sense, smiling under Utah's unambiguous sun. If Joseph Smith had money-digging, ball gazing, and other folk magical tendencies, who says that the Lord and Moroni couldn't still use him as an instrument and transform him? If God worked only through the impeccable, how could His

·

work be done on earth? Many would rather not deal frontally in any case with Smith's preposterous claims about the angel Moroni, the Hill Cumorah, the gold plates, and "Revised Egyptian." For it becomes apparent, talking to ordinary people in Salt Lake City and Provo and St. George and other great Mormon historical centers in Utah that many Mormons are members of their church for the social and moral milieu it provides and not for the sake of the more preposterous reaches of its theology. And some are there of course for the powerful commercial connections.

In the old days, when Saints were sent from Salt Lake to colonize other regions—St. George, for example, down south near the Arizona border and the marvels of Zion and Bryce Canyon, or down to harsh Moab in the canyons of the San Juan, or out into Arizona or Idaho— they were expected to pack up at once, sell their goods hurriedly, and depart. Through such outreachers, Mormonism has an influence in its surrounding states. Up in Wyoming one in ten of the population is Mormon. In Arizona the ratio is slightly less, but in Idaho it's nearly one in three.

The "mission"—the sending forth—is looked upon as the basis of Mormonism's success. Every businessman and solid citizen you meet in Salt Lake or Provo or St. George has been on his mission to England, South America, Australia, even the Bronx. The mission, as the Mormon historian Leonard J. Arrington acknowledges, was the mark of Joseph Smith's Mormonism and distinguished it from other nineteenth century marginal sects. It brought in new blood from Britain, Germany, and Scandinavia.

At a gas station in Flagstaff, I began to speak to a

well-dressed, muscular man about skiing—I was wearing
a ski cap which said Park City. He told me he had been
down to Black Canyon City to visit a nephew who'd just
returned from a mission to Brazil. "I think a guy like that
has something to tell me," the man announced.

And Brazil, that nation of woes, is closer in character
to a nineteenth century England or Scandinavia, the
countries from which the Mormons drew the new talent
who gave them their Deseret impetus.

I have seen Mormon missionaries moving through
the suburbs of my own hedonist hometown, Sydney—
clean, scrubbed boys in black pants, black ties, and drip-
dry shirts. They don't seem to enjoy eminent success, but
then Australia is a godless place, founded as a gulag during the Age of Enlightenment, having little of the tradition of religious fervor and revivalism which prevails still
in the U.S. and marks it as one of the most actively religious nations in the world.

B UT AT the center of the outreach is home, Temple
Square, with its great zeppelin-shaped tabernacle,
built at the end of the Civil War for social and cultural
meetings and for general church conferences. To anyone
who knows how little acoustic design went into most
nineteenth century public buildings, who has sat through
concerts in the New World's town and city halls and
listened to the meaningless crenellations of the roof and
walls bounce back garbled and fragmented and self-echo-
ing music, the tabernacle is a wonder. The great choir
resonates like a bell during Thursday night rehearsals
there and then on Sunday sings out in perfect pitch to

•

the world through a chain of Mormon-owned radio and television stations.

The Salt Lake City Temple, from whose pinnacle the angel Moroni blows his trumpet eastwards towards the trains of Saints emigrating from the godless plurality of Yankeedom, is the ultimate shrine however, a startling building even amongst all the big-city architecture of the business district. Aldous Huxley once called it—not without a gibe—"the Chartres of the Desert." A hundred years ago, it must have been dominant in the landscape of the basin. Though it had the traditional spires of conventional New England churches, it was also based on Joseph Smith's Temple at Nauvoo. It is shut to all but church members, because the most serious business is done here—as Arrington says, the divine and human meet, spiritual endowments descend on the Saints, people marry "for time and eternity," and ancestors are covenanted in. It was raised throughout the 1850s at great economic and physical cost.

In the Temple courtyard too, as well as the bell of the Nauvoo Temple brought on the long passage from the Mississippi, is found a memorial to seagulls. The Saints' harvest in 1848 was of enormous importance, because it was meant to stretch, to feed some two thousand extra Saints due to arrive from Missouri and from the Mormon winter quarters, situated in the present state of Omaha.

An odious black mass of crickets, however, descended on the Mormon crop. They'd been devouring it for some hours when a flock of seagulls arrived. The seagull is not unknown around Salt Lake, but it turned up that day in unprecedented numbers—an eyewitness said in numbers which blocked the sun. The crickets were themselves devoured, and the crop saved. So bountiful

•

was it that Brigham was able to dispatch wagonloads of food eastward to meet incoming Mormons who might be famished.

The seagulls were of course a sign that the Lord intended the Saints to occupy the region, which Brigham wanted to call *Deseret*. You still see that name everywhere in Utah, on the banner of the *Deseret News*, the church's newspaper, on banks, insurance buildings, mills, printeries, tire companies. "They did also carry with them deseret," says chapter two of the Book of Ether, "which, by interpretation, is a honey bee; and thus they did carry with them swarms of bees . . ."

Brigham wanted Deseret to encompass everything from the Oregon border to Mexico, from the Rockies to the Sierra Nevada. To provide a settlement on the sea, a beachhead, a colony of Saints were settled at Yerba Buena near the Pacific, a Californian enclave.

Brigham's plan for Deseret suffered some shrinkage however. Yerba Buena had to be abandoned, having lost many apostate Saints to mineral fever. In the beautiful, adobe Palace of the Governors in Sante Fe, a personable Yankee general named Tom Kearny had taken the surrender of all the region then named New Mexico or New Spain from a distraught Mexican official. And Utah itself was no longer simply the core of Deseret. It was now part of the United States.

I've already talked about how the fascinating tension between the Mormon and the Gentile, between the Salt Lake theocracy and the federal government, began early in Utah and how it still gives life in Utah its unique calibration.

Brigham and the Saints were not averse in principle

to the Gentiles or to trading with them and extending them kindnesses. In the flush of their seagull-led recovery, the Saints sold excess produce to Gentile wagon trains for premium prices but frequently nursed the ill.

There was a problem in that many California-bound folk brought with them prejudices against Mormonism. The worst instance of Mormon retaliation against Gentiles was directed at a wagon train whose members profaned Mormonism, made indecent suggestions to Mormon wives, and trampled Mormon crops.

At the time of the resultant Fancher massacre, President Buchanan had sent in U.S. troops from Wyoming to enforce the installation of various federal officials he had appointed, and there was panic in some of the Mormon settlements, a fear that the children of Israel were about to be obliterated.

It was in this atmosphere that the Fancher party, made up of good Missouri Mormon-haters and their families, camped at Mountain Meadows near Cedar City in the south of Utah. Brigham's adopted son, Major John D. Lee, commander of Mormon militia, orchestrated an attack by Ute Indians upon the train. When the Fancher party surrendered, the Mormon militia escorted the women and children out of the camp, and Lee placed a Mormon militia man at the side of every male member of the Fancher party. "Halt! Do your duty!" called this husband of nineteen Mormon women, and 129 men, women, and children were either instantly shot or killed off by Ute descending on them from the trees.

Brigham had no hand in or knowledge of this, and Major Lee was forced to portray it to him as an Indian massacre. And years later, to ease Utah's advance to

•

statehood, Lee was delivered up to a firing squad—still the prescribed means of execution in Utah, as Norman Mailer lets us know in *The Executioner's Song*.

You get the impression in modern Utah that the Gentile–Mormon relationship is still uneasily poised between the care and kindness offered to those traveling through, symbolized by the seagull memorial, and the mistrust represented in an extreme form by the Fancher business. A handsome Gentile woman in Park City complained rightly or wrongly that if she moved her business to Provo or Cedar City or one of the other "heavy Mormon towns," she could not hope to succeed. If the Mormons do look after their own, though, one should not be too surprised, for a special history like theirs, and a life marked by religious and social intensity, would inevitably encourage mutual aid and clannishness. In that regard, the Mormons would not be unique amongst sects and semisecret societies.

However, the them-and-us passions which operate on both parties to the Utah theocracy make of Utah a strangely divided society, an Ulster of the Southwest, even though violence on an Ulster scale is unlikely.

There is no other state like Utah. No other state ever had a prophet like Brigham. He was a genius of the human impulse toward producing a geographic exodus as a model for a spiritual exodus.

HAVING PICKED up in Salt Lake and read a little book of some of Brigham's sermons, I was disappointed with the one delivered by the Mormon preacher Spencer Kinard on the last Sunday of January in the Salt

Lake Mormon Tabernacle. By comparison with Brigham, it was an unexceptionable item of pulpit oratory such as might have been heard in any nonconformist church throughout America. Kinard quoted Oswald Spengler on the signs of declining nations. He asked whether Americans still held fast to the ideals of the Declaration of Independence and the Constitution; whether they still had a burning fervor of patriotism and emotion for "who we are as a people and a nation."

Compare the insipidity of such a homily with the great pugnacious homilies of Brigham. "I will say to our government, if they could hear me, 'You need never fight the Indians, but, if you want to get rid of them, try to civilize them.' How many were here when we came? At the Warm Springs, at this little grove where they would pitch their tents, we found perhaps three hundred Indians; but I do not suppose there are three of that band alive now . . . Did we kill them? No, we fed them. We brought their children into our families and nursed and did everything for them that it was possible to do for human beings, but die they would."

What about the pungency of this sermon about livestock contributions to the church? "Once in a while you would find a man who had a cow he considered surplus. Generally she was of the class that would kick a person's hat off, or eyes out, or the wolves had eaten off her teats. You would once in a while find a man who had a horse that he considered surplus, but at the same time he had the ringbone, was broken-winded, spavined in both legs, had the pole evil at one end of the neck and a fistula at the other and both knees sprung!"

Speaking of one of the early heretics of Mormonism, Howley, Brigham recounted during worship: "I put my

•

pants and shoes on, took my cowhide, went out and, laying hold of him, jerked him around and assured him that if he did not stop his noise and let the people enjoy sleep without interruption, I would cowhide him on the spot, for we had the Lord's prophet right here and we did not want the Devil's prophet yelling around the streets."

Kinard is at the end of the twentieth century deliberately pursuing a more anodyne line than Brigham ever felt any need to. But then Brigham never had a public affairs office, while the Mormon church today, like every other institution, does. The same color and ambiguities, heroisms and chicaneries go on beneath the surface, but the public voice of America, from congress to corporations to great evangelical movements, has been tidied up, and in the case of Sunday sermons in the tabernacle, deprived of the Byzantine vividness which is the stuff of Mormonism.

E VEN TODAY, though, in fact, probably more than in Brigham's day, there is a sort of proselytizing sweetness amongst the faithful, something I used to notice in young nuns and seminarians in my childhood, an institutionally loyal desire to project the inevitably superior wholesomeness, haleness, and joy which comes from the chosen path. I have to confess that I felt fully at ease only in the mountains, in places like Alta and Park City, General Connor's mineral towns where the Gentile character has always been strong. I confess this without pride and certainly without prejudice. With Mormonism as with all straitened sects, there is a tendency to depict the world as simpler than it is, to assert that all righteousness is in orthodoxy. Park City is a relief from that worldview.

I would say I was therefore a child of Connor if he hadn't been such a bigot. In any case, Park City *is* his child. I mentioned earlier that he is famous in Utah for deliberately seeking a mineral boom. He was in a way a worthy counterweight to the Saints, in that he like they was not pursuing his aim for mere reasons of commerce but for the sake of ideology. As he writes, "I have bent every energy and means of which I was possessed, both personal and official, towards the discovery and development of the mining resources of the Territory, using without stint the soldiers of my command wherever it could be done without detriment to public service."

It was when soldier miners were hacking out a fifty-foot trench in the Park City region that a speculator offered them $5,000 on the spot. From the Park City lodes would eventually come over $400 million worth of silver—in the values of the day, incalculable fortune, something equivalent of $120 billion. George Hearst, father of William Randolph Hearst, would be one who would participate in the Park City booms, as in many others.

Gentiles who did well there though, like Tom Kearns, the silver baron of Park City, would often move into Salt Lake with their wealth and temper its monoculture. Kearns and his partner, David Keith, a Nova Scotian who had worked with a Chinese rail gang on the Central Pacific, were able to build mansions a block apart on East South Temple, within sight of Moroni, whose angelic blasts made no impact on Kearns's Irish Catholicism or Keith's functional Presbyterianism. There Kearns held parties for his former Irish workmates, who in sober

Utah, a state which even today is scrupulous in its liquor laws, would reel home to Park City with their pockets full of bottles of Tom's champagne.

In Salt Lake, if you want wine with dinner, you have to make a special request, and the sense you get in some of the hotels is that you are breaking the normal surface of Salt Lake good order. In Park City the waiter himself will ask if you want wine. Even so, to go to a bar you have to pay a joining fee. There was a time when this restriction, this payment of a fee, this chosen enlistment in the armies of darkness, served as a barrier to hold back the righteous. Now it's just an inconvenience for people who come to Utah to ski or do business.

In the Park City museum and the town histories available in the book shop, space is given to photographs of Mother Urban, the two hundred pound Madam, who, with the help of twenty-five personable "seamstresses," kept Park City's enormous population of bachelors in a state of sexual composure. Similarly Archer, the under-taker, who during prohibition, used to run booze in from Wyoming in coffins, is acknowledged. Supreme in the museum, though, is Susanna Bransford, who married the Park City postmaster. He was a company secretary who held shares both legitimately and nominally, for purposes of deception, and who got wealthy thereby almost by ac-cident. When he died of alcoholism, she took over his mining affairs. By 1902 she was worth $100 million. She married Colonel Holmes, a lumber man and miner, in the Waldorf Astoria, and her dinner parties there and at large in New York and in Washington were, as she said, *"Creme de la creme* affairs *par excellence."* Holmes bought her Amelia Palace, the gothic mansion Brigham Young had built for his favorite wife. When Holmes died,

•

Susanna married a Serbian named Delitch, a brooding, jealous man, some thirty years her junior, who suicided in his cabin on an Atlantic liner after she had dismissed him and sent him off on a therapeutic cruise.

Now she married an emigré Russian prince named Engalicheff and relished signing herself into hotels as "HRH Princess Engalicheff." She outlasted Engalicheff, of course, and lived on in the company of a young business manager. She lunched with the widow of the silver baron, Thomas Kearns, and noticed that Mrs. Kearns still wore her wedding ring. "I hang mine in the bathroom, like grapes!" she told Mrs. Kearns.

She died at the age of eighty-three, in 1942, and by that time her fortune had sunk to some $60,000. Like Baby Doe she came in some ways, certainly in terms of silver booms, from a vaster, more staggering time than that in which she died.

IN THE 1950s, the population of Park City got as low as 1,500. The last mine closed in 1972. But already by then the population was increasing. Again, the new and supposedly endless industry was to be skiing. The Wasatch Mountains, amongst whose steep alpine meadows Park City lay, got reliable snowfall. The town ski-lift rises side by side with the no longer used towers of the old ore tramway. There are people in town who believe that both sets of towers will fall into desuetude, that the snow is growing unreliable. Everyone in the town talked about the lighter snows of the last winter of the 1980s, first winter of the 1990s in which I was traveling. There was a lot of, "It's not like the seasons of ten years ago.

•

They're having to use snow-making more than ever. The place was barely skiable at Christmas."

By Australian standards though, there nonetheless seemed plenty of snow up there. The U.S. ski team moved its headquarters there, to a complex on the west side of Park City. At Jeremy Ranch, a great cross-country Nordic ski set of trails was laid down.

Jeremy is very beautiful—black pinon pine on white hills and the mountains behind. It is a classic Western ranch, and unexorcised of its ghosts, either the ghosts of cowboys or of Ute, since the human traffic through those hills is so sparse and so genial. One late afternoon, on a six mile loop, we were passed there by a racer in a body stocking skating along on racing skis at a pace more appropriate to a car than a human. It seemed only a few minutes before he passed us again in the other direction, having got to the end of the loop and turned. In their colored body costumes and roaring across the slopes of snow-dusted mesquite, the racers move like heroes out of comic books, with a preposterous authority and speed. Back at the Nordic hut, they told us that the man who had swept past us twice was a coach of the U.S. Olympic Nordic team.

None of this region is far from Brigham's Emigration Canyon, the road into Deseret for the Saints. It is all such sublime country. Maybe religion is so strong in this landscape because this is terrain which puts the human in his place in a way Manhattan never could. You can come to a place like the Wasatch Mountains or the Great Salt Basin to learn your true scale.

THERE ARE forces working for the "Americaniza-
tion" of Utah other than the Gentile ethos of Park
City. Utah, like so much of the Southwest, Arizona and
New Mexico in particular, devotes a large part of its desolation to air bases and experimental ranges. The Hill Air
Force Range, the Wendover Range, the Desert Test Center, and the Dugway Proving Grounds are all to the west
and southwest of the Great Salt Lake. Much further
south, in remote Millard County, is the Desert Range
experimental station.

If you go to Wendover by way of Interstate 80, you
are surrounded by restricted areas of unexplained purpose. The same is true on the other side of the Great Salt
Lake, in the vicinity where in the nineteenth century the
two great railways, Union Pacific and Central Pacific met.
Morton Thiokol, the technology company responsible for
the O-rings in the ill-fated Columbia space shuttle, occu-
pies a long string of low hills and mesas here, northwest
of Brigham City, along the north side of the Great Salt
Lake. It is likely that if humankind goes to Mars in the
new century and ensures the survival of the species, if
not the settlement of the earth's griefs, by begetting children there, in that landscape rather like these low hills,
that Morton Thiokol will have a hand in it.

North of the Great Salt Lake and into Idaho, in the
square of land north of Tremonton and Logan, a region
into which I stumbled by accident, there are idyllic farming valleys, richly irrigated. Brigham would look on these
and approve of them as a model of Deseret. But half an
hour westward stands the desolation in which the defense
technocrats pursue their purposes.

Utahns often complain that the Air Force unilaterally
declares the wilderness a wasteland. The Air Force is

•

nonetheless a vast employer in Utah, as is the military throughout the West. Salt Lake City's Chamber of Commerce got very anxious about the reduction of squadrons at Hill Air Force Base north of the city. Yet the state as a whole fought the Air Force's attempt to introduce what is called "the MX racetrack basing system" for missiles, for it would have taken up a large part of the Great Salt Basin and would have made Utah even more of a nuclear target than it already is. The First Presidency of the Mormon Church, always eager to appease the feds, itself voted against the nuclear racetrack. Under pressure from Utahns and others and with a change of administration, the Defense Department abandoned MX and went on to embrace other Cold War strategies. But to travel in the West in the winter in which the Cold War was said to have ended made one all the more conscious of the enormity of land the U.S. Department of Defense has taken to itself.

•

FIVE

The Basin-and-Land-of-Dixie Blues

PROMONTORY IS as forlorn a place as appropriate, as western-looking as any aged child, bred on the old Western movies and visiting it for the first time, could hope for. It is named for the promontory which juts outward to the south into the Great Salt Lake. It is itself a classic desert bowl between snow-streaked hills. It is weirdly splendid with the winter snow on it. It has that wistful air of a place which American passion, greed, and enterprise once made the center of things, before moving on and taking other routes.

It was spring when the golden spike was driven at the place called Promontory Point in 1869. Engraved on the spike were these words: "May God continue the unity of our Country as this Railroad unites the two great Oceans of the world." What cheek, what spunk, what energy went into that spike! Amongst those who watched it driven were former engineers from the Union army,

•

Irish and German laborers, and some of the ten thousand Chinese who had made the Central Pacific's grade through the Sierras. The big photograph: The engineer of Locomotive 60, *Jupiter*, of the Central Pacific stands holding a bottle of champagne in the direction of Locomotive 119 of the Union Pacific. On the cowcatcher of 119, a triumphant laborer is waving two bottles of something or other, probably not lemonade. In the foreground, the piratical Central Pacific's Leland Stanford, who would leave his name on other railroads and on a university, shakes hands with Grenville Dodge, and the emigrant faces crowd around, staring at the camera.

Though there is only one possibly Chinese face on the Central Pacific side of the last spike, it was the Central Pacific's engineer Charlie Crocker's Chinese who had carried up the last tie.

According to charters issued by the federal government, each railroad was able to claim enormous acreages around each mile of track it laid. So the hills around Promontory still carry the visible signs of an astounding capitalist energy outlaid during the late winter and early spring of 1869. The Irish and Germans of the Union Pacific met up with the Chinese of the Central Pacific, and both kept going, on orders, right past and parallel to each other, acquiring land for their railroad—all according to statute—as they went. Their parallel cuts can be seen all the way from Promontory back eastward along Route 83 to the present main northern road out of Brigham City. There are thirty-two miles of late-winter cuttings and levelings. Both construction armies engaged in jovial racial wars against each other, the Irish laying dynamite charges by apparent accident in the path of the Chinese, the Chinese rolling rocks on the Irish. At last the

•

federal government itself called an end to this parallel cutting war and caused both railways to backtrack and join up at this spot amongst the Promontory Mountains, north of the Great Salt Lake.

It is believed that one of the reasons the railway took this route, along the Platte River through Nebraska, to Cheyenne, Laramie, Fort Fred Steele in Wyoming and down to Ogden in Utah, was the hope of exploiting rich Mormon traffic between Utah and Sacramento. Stanford had been in Utah the year before, drumming up business and freight contracts with Brigham and enlisting industrious Mormon work teams to do some grading east and west of Ogden. Many of the Mormons were nervous of the railway, but Brigham was characteristically forthright about it. "I wouldn't give much for a religion which could not withstand the coming of the railroad."

He had nonetheless wanted to get statehood before the railway arrived, so that the Saints, as distinct from the Union, could control the territory.

Promontory, in these melancholy hills which hone the wind to razor sharpness, is a place where there were once saloons and a township standing amidst the spring mud; where young tarts anxious to build their own nest of capital opened their arms to the hard-worked crews, some of the women "not even refusing the attention of the coolies;" where profligate energy was so intensely, cheaply, and bloodily applied. Now there is only an ornamental mile or so of track commemorating a stretch where Crocker's coolies, one record-breaking day in 1869, laid ten miles of the thing. Descendants of these crews make up the Chinese population of Salt Lake City. Much further east, before the Central Pacific got this far and was still in the Sierras above Donner Lake, tunneling and driving track across the summit, avalanches tore hundreds of Chinese down the mountainside, burying them till spring in the valleys below.

All for very little ultimate effect. Because Promontory was superceded. Other routes from coast to coast were soon negotiated further south—the Atlantic and Pacific Railroad, for example, which took a line through Flagstaff, Arizona, to Santa Fe and then up along the line of the old Santa Fe trail.

What is interesting about the joining at Promontory was that Americans seemed to have understood well at the time not only that the railroad made everything different but what sort of differences it would make. The American press and a number of politicians and commentators said it was an end to the West, and in a way it was. It certainly put an end to certain staples of our mythology of the West. The Pony Express, which ran bravely from station to station through the Four Corners area, carrying two saddlebags of highly priced mail, was dead now after a very short life. The Union Pacific had until now been forced to bring all its iron from the East by way of Cape Horn. Now California was connected to the East's iron.

And if the Saints had ever had a dream of leading an existence free of the influence of Washington and the Gentiles, the driving of the spike at Promontory finished it.

This northwestern corner of Utah is lonely, vacant, but somehow handsome. Wide sagebrush and mesquite-studded plains rimmed by blue-grey mountains called the Goose Creek and Grouse Creek Ranges, support a minute human population, perhaps the lowest density in the entire United States; a few five house and post office towns

•

made by the vanished rail or the marginal cattle ranching. In summer it would be a terrible country to drive in. You can see even in winter the possibilities of heat, the latent fire, in those broad, alkali-streaked valleys. But in winter the color of it all is exciting and subtle, and melancholy in a stimulating sort of way.

If there is anyone visible in Kelton or Lynn or Grouse Creek or Etna, you get a wave and an unambiguous smile from them, as if the United States was still a neighborly place. On Route 30, after the town of Rosette, it is eighty miles until you see another house, which turns out to be a cowboy bar in the barely existent Montello, Nevada. A long way in an eerie landscape. A long way even for an Australian.

IF THE Salt Basin northwest of Utah is so desolate, the south is a zone of awesomeness of a different kind and nearly as climatically severe. Brigham dispatched Mormon settlers down here, and you can tell it took a great deal of conviction and stubbornness to make something of it. The terrain of the south is not wide, alkaline desert but part of a great, complicated system of canyons, reefs, and mountains. It is riven by the enormous, dramatic reaches of the Green, Colorado, and San Juan Rivers. This country, around Dixie and Capital Reef, Canyonlands, Moab, and Monticello, was a bitter portion for the Saints.

Some of the townships bear a powerful resemblance to Alice Springs, the frontier town at Australia's center. Kanab could be dropped in the Australian wilderness and fit in perfectly, though again the Australians might find it an imposition to have to drive down to Fredonia, Arizona, for their liquor.

Given that I've already confessed to a tendency to be scared of immense landscapes like this, I was comforted to find a quotation on the wall of the visitor's center in the Canyonlands National Park, from the report of a park officer named Ranger Brown who looked down into the maze of the Canyonlands in the 1930s. "Do you recall that first terrifying revolt of our physical bodies at being subjected to such an overwhelming and unaccustomed scale of landscape as we look down—down into the abyss of that writhing cataclysm? Back in normal surroundings, it is easy to smile in recollection of the violent denial that rose within us as the shock of that scene pounded through our veins, as if the once too insolent flesh was protesting over this sudden dwarfing comparison of its puniness . . ."

The Fremont people abandoned southern Utah round about 1000 A.D., possibly under pressure from a new Uto-Aztecan people called the Paiute, and the remaining Paiute still live down there, in St. George and other towns.

The Paiute were and still are a race of basket makers and potters, and they may have taken the habit of farming from the Fremont. If this account is full of sad stories of what befell the unfortunate of the West, not one account will surpass that of the Paiute for sadness.

The sadness is perhaps more acute too because we know that in the Zion area they too felt the same landscape-awe as Ranger Brown did, as Edward Abbey confessed to, and as had power to make me flinch and cower when in the open or behind the steering wheel of my four-wheel drive. Even the extraordinary tunnels on

•

Route 9 into Zion, long, long tunnels with openings punched in them to allow glimpses of the Great Arch and the East Temple, are in tone with the massive scale of the landscape. Of course they break Edward Abbey's dictum that the only way to enter such wonders as Zion and Arches National Parks is on your hands and knees.

The Paiute would not stay in Zion Canyon after dark. At the mouth of the Narrows of the canyon, they named a rock for their wolf god, Sinawava, and he was their spiritual anchor in the enormity of this country, letting them enter here in the hope of an assured return.

Their first contact with Europeans, at least that we know about, was with the remarkable Franciscan friar, Domingeuz Escalante. Anyone traveling in the Four Corners region keeps on running up against Escalante's name. The friar was involved in an attempt to find a road to Monterey from the Spanish town of Santa Fe on the Rio Grande. He worked his way through the Rockies northward into Colorado and then into Utah, taking a more southerly route than Brigham's immigrant train would. The terrain and the season and the ceaseless watch required against understandable Ute aggression forced him to return via this southeastern part of Utah and through northern Arizona to Santa Fe again. Escalante's journey began just before the signing of the Declaration of Independence and was completed within that revolutionary year, 1776. Captain Cook was in the South Pacific, and the Americans had not yet conceived of Manifest Destiny, and the gold tablets of Mormon's book still slept in the Hill Cumorah.

The Paiute, as a gentle, congenial, unhorsed and semisedentary group of indigenes, having seen their first Spaniard would thereafter become a favorite target of

•

Spanish and Mexican slave dealers working from Santa Fe and supplying the market in the Chihuahua and Sonora provinces of Mexico.

A thousand or so Paiute survive in a poor settlement near Cedar City, Utah. They have suffered from not having any treaty with Washington upon which to base claims for equity. They were disqualified from all Federal benefits in 1956. One writer notes, "Without birth certificates, Social Security numbers, or land deeds, they couldn't collect welfare or negotiate loans. For that matter, they didn't even know how to qualify for hunting and fishing licenses to seek food in the mountains and streams of their forefathers."

When the federal government "emancipated" the Paiute in this way, their lack of standing in the connecting world of contract-making and benefit-receiving meant they had to call on local banks to sell their land. The Indian Peaks band, who lived beneath the Needle Range in the inevitably named Escalante Desert, sold all their reservation land in the late 1950s for $40,000.

But wait, for the grief is not yet fully recounted. The ancient craft of basketry, practiced in modern time by a declining number of Paiute women, suffered a fatal impact as the use of chemical agents and pesticides by farmers and government people in this region increased. The Paiute basket makers trim willows by dragging them through their teeth, and such was the concentration of DDT in the fronds of willow, many of them became gravely ill. The few left now go by car as far as Central Nevada to find willows uncontaminated by chemicals.

Paiute religion was overborne by Mormon religion, and in Cedar City and down in northern Arizona, many

•

of the Paiute are baptized Mormons, smiling the indefatigable Mormon smile in truckstops and motels or wherever they are employed. The Laminite children turning home again, embraced by the latter day Nephites!

IT WAS a Mormon scout Isaac Behunin who named Zion, and Nephi Johnson who penetrated its canyon, having left behind his Paiute guide who justifiably feared Wai-no-Pits, the consuming deity of the place.

The Mormons, Brigham specifically, had already called the area between Cedar City and Capital Reef, Dixie. It was to be a "cotton mission." Just south of St. George, where, when I was passing through, the city council was trying to run a hippie shopkeeper out of town because he had decorated his display window with two inanimate figures locked together clumsily to represent copulation, there is a Mormon petroglyph on the side of the road. It reads, "Jacob Peart Jr I was sent her to rais cotton march 1858."

Peart probably did well enough, because St. George is a solid town. But those who occupied canyons like Zion were swept away by flash floods and fevers. Even Mormon endurance didn't avail. Zion, like enormous and barely habitable Bryce Canyon further east, reverted to being what it is manifestly intended to be: a mere wonder.

A Methodist minister, Frederick Vining Fisher, named many of the peaks of Zion in the early twentieth century. Eurocentrically, he dubbed them in terms of his own culture, following the lead of the U.S. Geological Survey, which had already spoken of the Western and Eastern

Temples and Towers of the Virgin. The Mormon settlers spoke of the West Temple in more earthy terms—Steamboat Mountain.

There is an enormous block of Entrada and Navajo sandstone which dominates the mouth of the Narrows, and Frederick Vining Fisher said of this, "It is by all odds America's masterpiece . . . I have looked for this mountain all my life but I never expected to find it in this world. This is the Great White Throne."

Likewise the ecclesiastically minded Fisher scattered names such as the Altar of Sacrifice, the Three Patriarchs, the Great Organ, and Angels' Landing across other formations, large and small, just as the Mormons themselves left a Mount Moroni. All of this seems a gallant effort to exorcise and gentle the unutterable landscape by clutching at one's own myths and theology, thereby attributing to God and rain and wind a sculptural intention. In Bryce, similarly, there are the Queen's Garden, Thor's Hammer, and where erosion of the softer lower layers in columns of stone leaves wider flatter slabs on top, the Hat Shop. It's all brave where it's not cute, but I am pleased to say it hasn't worked.

Zion stays as threatening and wonderful, as do the upthrust heights and downthrust canyons of Bryce. If you are a bored American, if you want to be provoked and frightened, overborne and reawakened, the rough parallelogram which lies between Interstate 70 and the Grand Canyon is the place to test yourself. Here none of the manufactured, plastic frights with which our culture kindly tries to purge our souls can be found. Here is nothing less than the sharp edge of the absolute, the experience which turned the Ranger Edward Abbey into the Elijah of monkey-wrenching. Yosemite and the Grand Tetons and Yellowstone are neighborly by comparison with this scary Utahn slab of geologic madness.

And of course if you want to see it as some Mormon conscript sent to Dixie saw it or as some Paiute fearful of Wai-no-pits, then—again—go in winter, when the fantastical earth is further defined by ledges of snow: There, more or less alone, you will see in Zion the Anasazi petroglyphs chipped out on slabs of that dark pigmentation called "desert varnish."

THE SAN Juan region in southeastern Utah was the last area settled by the Mormons. Brigham sent out scouts in 1871. It is the corner of Utah which is separated from the rest by the north–south slantwise descent of the Colorado River. Moab, its biggest town, is—as the locals like to say—the "gateway" to Arches and Canyonlands, even though Arches and most of Canyonlands are on the north rim of the river. Both places are the river's children and part of the same grotesque geology as San Juan.

For example, the whole valley of Moab, we're told to put us in our place, was once a seabed where a slab of salt lay, the size of Connecticut and two to three miles thick. Flues of salt rose up under pressure of rock, and when it rained and the salt dissolved, the rock it held fell in on itself.

Salt then, the great desolator and the great preserver of the dead, is all too credible a maker of the savage portion which Brigham named Moab after another Biblical wasteland. Moab, the land beyond Jordan. The Mormons hadn't known that, beside the Colorado, the Jordan was a homely stream.

·

THE ARCHES for which the nearby park of that name is famous are created by later erosions of sandstone, helped by heat, wind, rain, and ice. Arches is so massive that again it seems almost criminal to give it such a cute name and try to diminish it. The forces which made this landscape were so immense that the arches themselves are only one minor geologic trick in a whole array of excessive effects, amongst them the ceaseless, mazed canyons which run north and east.

In this canyon country, east of Salina, and approaching the Green River on its way through profound Gray Canyon to feed into the Colorado, I was pulled over for exceeding the speed limit. I don't know what my excuse was. You can't tell a cop that you're speeding because you have found the country too overpowering. When we both stopped, the sheriff got down from his glittering truck. In New York, the police cars affect the same battered and stained appearance as the city's taxis, but out here, even on the edge of nothingness, the sheriffs' vehicles glitter and are undented. No traffic or miscreant has managed to take the gloss off them. They are arrayed with lights in the national colors. Three cheers for the red, white, and blue. The rectitude of the great republic shining through the noonlight and dead of night.

It was very possible he was a Mormon, a true son of that other tough man, Brigham. He moved with the appropriate lazy threat a sheriff should show. Did the movies get it from men like this, or did men like this get it from the movies? The country was okay for him. Arches was just Arches. The great gorges of the Green,

Colorado, and San Juan were just places where he fished. Newspaper Rock, a desert-varnished section of the Windgate Cliffs, covered with petroglyphs of all kinds, even those of U.S. Cavalry men and fleeing polygamists as well as those of the holy Anasazi, was just Newspaper Rock. A bunch of graffiti.

He was no more frightened by where he was then Butch Cassidy was the time he hijacked the Colorado River Ferry near Moab on his way back to one of his hiding places in unplumbable Capitol Reef.

The sheriff thought I'd hadn't been quick enough in pulling over. "Do you know what a red flashing light means?" he asked. "Do you speak English?"

He would have thought that I was a smart aleck if I'd said that in the general glitter of that terrain his red light had looked, to me, an irrelevance. But he was very lenient once he knew what I was, a foreigner. A foreigner from a country which he surmised was rather like this. A country which you tried to get under control by spraying and damming it somewhat, by laying familiar and diminishing names to it. For Ayers Rock, for example, was as silly and partial a name for Australia's central primeval monolith as Arches or Capitol Reef for the places they were attached to.

AROUND HERE it is not only the great rifts in the earth and the bizarre erosions that test the visitor. It is the ultimate authority of the La Sal Range. The Mountains of Salt. If the snow-filled depths don't get you, the snow-peaked heights will. The La Sal was the scene of an abortive and grievous mineral rush in the 1960s, the one which the eccentric ranger-novelist Edward Abbey would satirize in *Desert Solitaire* and a string of other books.

Abbey was a remarkable, misanthropic environmental prophet who worked a great deal in, and wrote a great deal about, this area. He died in 1989 and is buried somewhere in the Sonoran Desert in Arizona. The spot is not marked. Even in death he isn't keen on tourists or motorized pilgrims. "The arguing of wilderness needs no defense," wrote Abbey. "It only needs more defenders."

He was an enemy of strip-mining in the San Juan, Colorado River areas, of its power to generate jobs that bring about ultimate degradation. The Navajo—whose reservation begins just south of the San Juan and then runs down into Arizona—were getting a royalty payment and a job for thirty-five years, he said, but their minor and short-term prosperity would be followed by the sort of desolation which characterizes Appalachia. "Meanwhile the Indians and everyone else living a hundred miles downwind of the present and projected power plants [Warner Valley, Escalante, Caineville—all in southern central Utah] will receive as a bonus a concentrated steady treatment of flying ash, sulphur dioxides, and nitrogen oxide."

He sometimes urged people to stay out of the wildernesses anyhow, if they could, whatever their purpose. "Why go there? Those places with hard case names: Starvation Creek, Poverty Knoll, Hungry Valley, Bitter Springs, Last Chance Canyon, Dungeon Canyon, Whipsaw Flat, Dead Horse Point, Scorpion Flat, Dead Man Draw, Stinking Spring, Camino del Diablo, Jornado del Muerto . . . ?"

His most famous novel was *The Monkey Wrench*

•

Gang, in which he dealt with a gang of environmental rebels. They went about the Southwest destroying unnecessary dams, loosening unnecessary bridges, dynamiting unnecessary power plants. In the West now you can find manuals of monkey-wrenching in most good bookshops. They urge you, for example, to drive nails of a certain length into threatened trees—nails that are not large enough to harm the tree but of sufficient strength to rip the teeth out of a saw.

Abbey says in one of his books that his first act of monkey-wrenching was the cutting down of the sign on the outskirts of Moab which proclaimed the town to be "The Uranium Capital of America."

He reserved his more acute jeremiads for the great national parks of America which, he believed, neutralized the wilderness by making everything too accessible. "Do not jump into your automobile next June and rush out to the Canyon country hoping to see some of that which I have attempted to evoke in these pages. In the first place you can't see *anything* from a car; you've got to get out of the goddamn contraption and walk, better yet crawl, on hands and knees, over the sandstone and through the thornbush and cactus. When traces of blood begin to mark your trail, you'll see something, maybe. . . . This is not a travel book but an elegy. A memorial. You're holding a tombstone in your hands. A bloody rock. Don't drop it on your foot—throw it at something big and glassy."

He inveighed against what he called *industrial tourism*: "Natural Bridges Moneymint or Zion National Parking Lot or General Shithead National Forestland of Many Abuses." Congress had directed the Park Service in 1916 to "provide for the enjoyment of same in such man-

•

ner and by such means as will leave them unimpaired
for the enjoyment of future generations." Edward Abbey
declared himself to be on the side of "leave them
unimpaired."

Having driven *and* then walked *and* then skied in
national parks in the Southwest, reluctantly, since I lack
hardihood and would rather have things easy, I must
agree with him. The Grand Canyon for example feels
too accessible. We know in our water we shouldn't be
permitted to whiz around its rim in such a cavalier way.
We're getting too much too easily for it to signify. The
reader is justified in laughing at hearing that sort of asser-
tion from a writer who has already confessed to the impulse to hide behind the wheel of his car when faced with
Canyonlands and Arches. But there *is* an unreality to the
vehicle. It separates us from the enormity and the slow
accretion and assimilation of the shocks of the landscape.
We go to the Grand Canyon and don't know we've been.

So Abbey called for no more cars in national parks.
He called for no new roads. He even turned on his col-
leagues and called for putting the park rangers to work.
"Lazy, scheming loafers, they've wasted too many years
selling tickets at tall booths and sitting behind desks fill-
ing out charts and tables in the vain effort to appease the
mania for statistics which torments the Washington Office. Put them to work. They're supposed to be rangers—
make the bums range."

Abbey's voice is frequently heard amongst people of
the Southwest. I met a devoutly middle class, very urbane
trekking operations manager who confessed that what he
would most like to do for humanity was to blow up the
Glen Canyon dam on the Colorado. I asked about the
dangers of anarchy and subjective judgment which plague

any such action. But a true monkey-wrencher says, "You can't make a mistake if you return to wilderness. And aren't the other guys being subjective too? Dressing it up as professional judgment but finding the data to justify their technical arrogance?"

Abbey and this region and the dams and all the rest of it raise the profoundest human question. Does the world exist for its own sake or for humankind's? Does it exist for the sake of both? Is humankind the peak of creation or the terminal virus?

To do Abbey justice, I think he came down potentially on both sides of every question, even this one, but he generally opted for the virus model.

Now he is happily returning to the desert somewhere among the giant saguaro cactus of the Sonora. He will certainly come back as an eagle. He will at least surmount the dams.

SIX

The Anasazi Solstice

HE THEME that changing climate might put an end to the skiiing boom was taken up by some people I met on the North Rim of the Grand Canyon. My wife and daughter and I drove on a snowy road south from Jacob Lake, having heard that a skimobile might be going into North Rim, where a Colorado summer rafter ran a Nordic, or cross-country, ski camp. He accommodated skiers in yurts erected next to the snow-submerged gas station and fed them in the park store.

The snowmobile was ready to go when we arrived, but it was still waiting for the rafter himself, the boss. So we waited too. When he turned up, he had a man from New Hampshire with him who turned out to be a designer of ski resorts. On the long way into North Rim, the designer and the rafter lamented the bad season then in progress, though to an Australian eye there again

•

seemed no shortage of snow. In fact, when we got to North Rim, we found the park gas station sign—a beacon in summer—buried to its neck.

Nonetheless, the designer said he was turning now exclusively to designing Nordic skiing centers. There was always reliable snow for that, even if the greenhouse effect did prove to be a reality, even if the temperatures rose a degree or two on average throughout the world. Downhill skiing was dependent partly on snow falling reliably on specific slopes. Whereas in a place like North Rim, there is so much room that there was always snow—if not in one arm of the forest then in another— and it ran for miles.

In the yurts we slept in doonahs on wooden benches and went down paths dug in shoulder-deep snow to a chemical lavatory in the woods. The wind howled, the sky was streaky, and though amongst the ponderosa pine we skied as hard as we could on the eighteen-mile loop between the village of North Rim and the rim itself, we got only a distant view into the canyon before the light began to go and fresh snow began slanting across our path.

Back at the yurts, satisfied with our effort, we met a party of five young men and women who, after a good meal at North Rim, were going to take off with three days' food and ski to the very rim. Then they would climb—on crampons and carrying their packs and skis— down the ice-covered trail along Bright Angel Canyon to Phantom Ranch at the very bottom of the Grand Canyon itself. From there they would ascend to the South Rim.

One of them was a lean English girl besotted with Arizona's spaciousness. Another of the party, a male, said that it creates a wonderful stir amongst the tourists on

•

the South Rim when you emerge over the edge of the abyss with your long, skinny skis strapped to your back.

When they left at daybreak one morning, we ourselves went off on a ski to a fire tower in the forest, but it seemed a Sunday stroll by comparison with their endeavor, especially since they had made it sound like a routine little hike anyhow, and since they apparently spent the summers running rapids in the Colorado and Green and the winters on ski excursions like this.

We knew that ultimately we were going to the South Rim (a prodigious distance by the way, since the Colorado is such a mighty rift). We would travel there tamely, by the method despised by Edward Abbey. Automobile.

WHEN THE federal government built the town of Page, Arizona, on the south bank of the Colorado, creating a town which would be a base for the raising of the Glen Canyon Dam itself, they were able to appropriate the area from the Navajo and give them in compensation equivalent amounts of land in northeastern Utah.

There has been a controversy about whether Page or the dam was necessary. It gave plenty of employment to Navajo, but the situation of that tribe, said the rafter (echoed by many a Navajo in the bars of Page), seems just as parlous as it did when dam construction began in the last 1950s.

The rafter who drove us back to the park entrance and whose grandfather and father were Colorado rafters too, hated the dam. He disbelieved and was affronted by the assertions which were made to people who visited it. "Before Glen Canyon Dam was built," says the dam literature, "the Colorado River ran warm and muddy red. Now it is clear and cold." It's cold, says the rafter, because it's goddam dead. "Today," claims the dam literature, "stocked rainbow trout thrive in the cold water, often reaching trophy size." An introduced fish in an artificial river, says the rafter.

"Before 1956, the land near the future damsite was virtually inaccessible. Even rafters and boaters could easily visit only the floor of the canyon."

Alleluia! says the rafter.

"Nearby Navajo Indians, who pastured livestock on meager desert grass in the area, suddenly found themselves near stores, schools and medical care. Many Navajos worked on the construction of the Glen Canyon Dam."

But Navajo of the Glen Canyon Dam region and of the town of Page, the town created by the building of the dam, are not happy about how their water rights have survived the dam and the uses it is put to. Here is an Indian statement on the matter. "In 1968 the power plant built to burn Black Mesa coal at Page, Arizona, needed cooling water. The Navajo Tribal Council was persuaded (some say forced) to make only a small claim on Colorado River water and then give two thirds of it away to the power company and the town of Page. The water that the tribe might have claimed and the water they actually gave away is worth millions to the people who use it now. The tribe may never get any of it back."

The rafter says it would have been a harder transaction if the Indian ground needed for Page and the dam had been one of those areas on which the ancient towns of North America stand, or else one of the long established pueblos of northern New Mexico, San Juan or Taos

•

or Santo Domingo. The Pueblo Indians have special title to their pueblos, far more secure in practice than Navajo title. The Americans at least look upon the Hopi and Pueblo as immovable. The Navajo however are expected to take land to the north for land to the south. To administrative minds, they are utterly mobile, and all their land and water is up for continual negotiation.

One of the other reasons the rafter hated the Glen Canyon Dam on the Colorado is that its flooding in 1963 destroyed six hundred Anasazi sites. Archaeologists were let in to record what was there, and then the water rose.

Nearly everyone who knows about them feels very comfortable with the idea of the Anasazi. For whether they lived in dwellings slotted beneath the brow of cliffs or on top of mesas, their life seems to have been communal in a way more akin to our lives, to have been sedentary and industrious in the European way.

You have only to look at the destiny of the Plains Indians or of the Australian aboriginals to know that there is something ideologically offensive to the European soul in nomadism. The Anasazi get marks for having been settlers and *settled*.

The Hopi and the Pueblo themselves are unabashed in telling you about the ancient superiority of *their* way over that of the Navajo and Apache. We were in conversation with a young man at the winter bean festival in the Hopi settlement of Walpi, probably the second oldest permanent settlement in America (circa 1100—though it did change its location by a mile or so around 1700 and sits now on the prow of south-pointing First Mesa). When we mentioned the Navajo, the young Hopi told us, "We taught them everything they know. Weaving and pottery and farming. But they aren't up to us in any of

•

125

it. Have you ever seen the kachinas they make? They're laughable."

No sectarian passion is profounder than the passion of the townsfolk for the wanderers, or the other way round. The one is a heresy against the other. The two do not contemplate each other calmly. The Hopi consider the Navajo as barely reformed nomads.

SO BACK to the Four Corners' chief emotional favor-ites, the Anasazi. The Four Corners area is full of the remains of this race. Right throughout the Colorado and its plateaus and canyons, down into Chaco and Canyon de Chelly and over to the mesas and cliffsides of south-western Colorado, the Anasazi immanence is everywhere. Vanished, they are still around. Norman Lopez told me the old Ute see them and communicate with them be-neath Ute Mountain in Colorado. In Arizona and Utah, they give messages to the Navajo. Their gods are amongst those who come back from the San Francisco mountains to the kivas on the Hopi mesas, including the kivas of Walpi, in the winter.

The horse cavalry and Butch Cassidy were a phase here. The Anasazi are a presence centuries deep.

America's ignorance of its *true* Indian history, as dis-tinct from its perceived one, the fatuous Indian history of the Western movie, may be a national tragedy. For it is inappropriate and dangerous to think you are a young country if in fact you are an old one. If you believe that the first American towns occurred in Virginia in the late sixteenth century, then you do not have a real history. But that is what most Americans *do* believe.

•

THE PLACE WHERE SOULS ARE BORN

In the Four Corners region you are continually beckoned by obscure little signs on secondary roads to towns which were old long before the Virgin Queen gave her name to any American colony. One of the places you are beckoned to coming southeast along the line of the San Juan toward Colorado is an Anasazi settlement called Hovenweep. It was not called Hovenweep by the Anasazi themselves, of course, but by the Ute, to whom Hovenweep means *abandoned valley*.

Again, we approached Hovenweep in winter. I want to avoid being toffee-nosed and arrogant about this winter business, since it is unlikely I would have had a mandate to go to Hovenweep in winter if Jan Morris hadn't asked me to write this book, but it is inevitable that winter will be more atmospheric, since ghosts *do* come out again once the Winnebagos return to their winter camps in Southern California or Jersey. The way to Hovenweep is over icy roads between pastures and black winter pinto bean fields with snow in the furrows. The roads mock the border. You can't keep track, approaching Hovenweep, of whether you're in Colorado or Utah, and it is a suitable irrelevance, since you have enlisted yourself in a preborder experience once the flat plateau breaks up and Cajon Mesa begins to be riven with canyons.

There have been what the anthropologists call in their whimsical way "Paleo-Indians" here for fourteen thousand years. Not to confuse the business of the Anasazi; but one heretical scholar has argued that the Paleo-Indians who lived in Hovenweep before the Anasazi are the ancestors of the Ute; that therefore the Ute did not come down ravening Yellow-Peril-wise from the Siberian Arctic to displace the Anasazi pueblo dwellers but were here always. That the Anasazi were the interlopers. This

•

127

would undercut the traditional reasons the Spaniards had for enslaving the Ute, the reasons which gave a color of justification to the U.S. cavalry in their war against the Ute and the Navajo.

Like Phoenix and Tucson, like all the wars waged in the Southwest, like all the land consortiums (Rings) and their hired guns, Hovenweep was centered upon water. The Anasazi themselves were there very early in the Christian era. They farmed the tops of Cajon Mesa, but then, about 1150, they moved to the heads of the valleys and built the wonderful towers you still come on so unexpectedly—across a flat finger mesa—at the beginnings of canyons. These were the same race of people as the ones who occupied Mesa Verde.

The canyons are not so steep here and there were no great rock overhangs into which to slot cliff dwellings of the kind you see in the Mesa Verde.

The Hovenweep people built exquisite drystone towers—Square Tower, Hovenweep Castle, Cajon Ruins, Unit Type House. They dry-farmed the tops of the mesas for perhaps a thousand years, from 100 A.D., and used irrigation to grow squash, corn, and beans in the canyon bottoms. Their check dams are everywhere throughout the heads of the canyons, built up of dry stone masonry and plugged with clay to hold the runoff from the mesa top. So they were practical farmers here for six or seven times longer than there have been white farmers in Kansas.

No one knows what the beautiful towers they built are for, the towers which give Hovenweep its superb ambience. We do know they dealt partly with astronomy. Their minimal windows led cowboys to believe that they were concerned with defense, but in fact they focus light against interior walls, which were once plastered and then painted and decorated with astronomical markers. What the windows do variously is direct against the far inner wall of the tower a beam of light at sunrise and sunset at the equinoxes, sunrise and sunset at the solstices—and at no other times of the year. The towers are, whatever else their purpose was, devices for focusing the light of the sun and giving the Anasazi farmer infallible signals as to when to undertake certain rituals and when to begin certain of the functions of farming.

The dry stonework of the towers is admirable enough. God knows what devices and measuring sticks were used to ensure that each of the towers gave the community such infallible signs of decline and burgeoning, of dawn on the shortest day and dusk on the longest!

A great distance from Hovenweep, in Newgrange in County Meath in the Republic of Ireland, there is a massive neolithic tomb which took thirty years to build and whose *raison d'etre* is similarly to focus the morning sun on the shortest day of the year through an aperture between two cope stones and so into a central chamber. In County Meath the sun rises on December 21 at two minutes before 9 A.M. A local man in Meath believes that the neolithic Irish farmers needed to concentrate that shaft of light into the burial chamber so that the souls of those departed the earth but still waiting in that night-black room could go now, as if hauling themselves toward another world on the long, strenuous beam. There is something remarkable in this—that Anasazi farmers like the ancient indigenes of Ireland obviously believed that the cap-

•

ture of light at solstices was essential to the management of their lives and their management of the world, temporal and spiritual.

THE HOVENWEEP people—with their towers and habitations and check dams at the heads of canyons—had relatives in Colorado's Montezuma Valley, which is just below Hovenweep and just over what is now the Colorado–Utah border. And both had further relatives on the enormous mesa called Verde, all of them admirable farmers, basket weavers, and potters.

Unlike Hovenweep, Mesa Verde is enormous in spread and height, a beetling and widespread tabletop. Just as the Three Mesas in northeastern Arizona is the known world and a self-supporting universe to the Hopi, Mesa Verde must have been something the same to these Anasazi, even though they may indeed have had contacts with people as far south as the Aztecs.

And so again I start to speak of this Southwestern business of space and scale: The climb up Mesa Verde, even by automobile, is a humbling affair. I was led to wonder if my passion for the Southwest was really an attempt to check my tendencies to vertigo, as already so heavily canvased in this account. The chief table-mountain mass of Verde is teased out into finger mesas as big as lower Manhattan. The escarpments are predictably stimulating and terrifying. One of the wintering rangers told me that Texans, who come from a flat state, have the greatest problems negotiating its switchbacks.

Going there in winter from a sort of residual Celtic belief that the ghosts come back then, we didn't have the comfort of a stream of vehicles to my front and rear. The roads were sheeted with ice whenever an escarpment rose above the tar, blocking the sun. It is all very well to go there looking for the spirits of a place, but most interesting when you begin to suspect you may become one yourself. Though the road might slot itself into a cliffside, the heights which fell away below the road were immensely greater than the ones that occasionally rose above it. If you went over there, someone in Cortez told us with a local-wit cheeriness, you'd roll all the way to Mancos.

I shall later dutifully visit the Grand Canyon South Rim, and find it exhilarating once I'm there. But this—Mesa Verde—is the center of the journey. There are a few places which once visited inhabit your dreams for decades as the desired land where all the elements are in a sublime balance. One such place was the Antarctic continent, which I visited in 1968. More than twenty years later I still dream of McMurdo Sound icebound, of the sea lions sunning like slugs amongst the upheaved ice slabs along the shore, of the fuming volcano Erebus rearing behind one's back, of the Royal Society Range across the sound, with the midnight sun five degrees above their summits and shining down the glittering length of its glaciers.

When I went back to Mesa Verde for two days in winter I had not seen the place for fifteen years, but again I knew it at once. It was like McMurdo. I had been there on what the aboriginals of the Western Desert of Australia called *badunjari*: dream journeys.

Two enormous finger mesas of Verde, one called Chapin and the other called Wetherill, attracted concentrations of Anasazi from about 600 A.D. onward. They farmed along the tops of the mesas, living for the early

•

131

centuries of their occupation in pit houses along the tabletops. Some of their villages were surrounded by wooden palisades. Each settlement probably based their identity on blood relationship and association with a particular religious lodge, since that is the situation with both the Hopi and the Pueblo in the last decade of the twentieth century. Far View on top of the north rim of Mesa Verde was a village of about four hundred people toward the end of the ninth century.

The Anasazi were here on Chapin and Wetherill for seven hundred years or so. What they call—in cricketing parlance—a decent innings. Their wattle-and-daub dwellings developed toward 900 A.D. into the classic abutted living apartments of the kind you still see in, say, Taos, New Mexico. But the pit houses, which were used for community debate and for lodge purposes and which developed into the kiva, were completely underground. The secular was above the surface, and the spiritual was subterranean.

A ROUND ABOUT the time of the Norman invasion of England, there were about thirty thousand people farming along the Montezuma Valley to the north of Mesa Verde, in the vicinity of the town of Cortez, and only a tenth of that number were living up here in mesa-top settlements. But the remains of mesa-top life have lasted in graphic form.

Like their relatives in Hovenweep, these people were energetic users of what they had on their tableland. Because it was arid farming up here amongst the juniper and piñon pine and yucca, they built a reservoir capable of holding a half-million gallons of water at Mummy Lake, a little to the north of Far View. You can still see the system of stone terraces, collection ditches, and canals. Their industry, like the industry of all vanished peoples, of all people who got a temporary and clever purchase over a difficult terrain, brings tears to the eyes. They fed their children, they made their way, they didn't stint with effort, and they had time to weave impeccable baskets and turn exquisite pots of black and white and highly stylized design. Sometimes they gave a basket-look to their pottery, indented its surface with sticks or with their thumbnails.

Down in the Montezuma Valley, an Anasazi town of two-and-a-half thousand people or so and eighteen-hundred rooms existed—its name was Yellow Jacket. But it is the cliff-dwelling houses the relatives of these valley residents moved into about the end of the eleventh century, the pueblos which still stand beneath the overhangs of Mesa Verde, that will always be associated with the name of honor: Anasazi.

THE MEN who found the cliff dwellings came here in winter too. They were two cowboys who had followed the trails of Benjamin Wetherill's strayed cattle up on to Mesa Verde. They were on that arm of it which would ultimately be called Chapin Mesa, looking in the snow at the hoof marks left by Wetherill's cows. They were in fact both young relatives of Wetherill, a Quaker rancher of Mancos. One was Wetherill's son Richard, the other was his son-in-law. Just as you do now, moving along surrounded by solid earth and illimitable juniper and piñon, they came out onto a platform of rock and saw the canyon below them—a canyon which would ultimately be called Cliff Canyon. Across it, through driving snow, they saw the beautiful apartments they would later call Cliff Palace, socketed in under the opposing canyon wall.

For a little while, until they climbed down to the place, they might have thought they'd found a new civilization. But the pueblo, when they got there, was empty. Though the last Anasazi had left it perhaps nearly six hundred years before, there were cooking pots on the hearth, pottery was strewn on the floor. Richard Wetherill mentions seeing sandals in the corner. As if the occupants had just stepped out.

That's the wonder of Cliff House and of Spruce Tree House and all the others. They possess that air of having been alive with activity until the second you look at them. Someone is lying low there.

Richard Wetherill, searcher for cows, now became possessed by the Anasazi. He spent a long time at Cliff Palace, Spruce Tree House, and Square Tower House collecting. He found the jars with corrugated surfaces; he found the beautiful black-on-white bowls and pitchers and ladles. He found black-and-white drinking mugs with handles—mugs which wouldn't be out of place in some coffee-crazed American office even now.

He became utterly absorbed and should have known better. But after a bitter winter of camping out and digging, berserk with admiration for the Anasazi and with hopes of a corresponding public excitement, he took his collection by wagon to the southwest Colorado town of Durango, a mining and railway town ultimately to become—by the end of the 1980s—a marginal ski resort.

•

He says that people in Durango disappointed him by considering his collection to be just "more Indian stuff."

His next effort was a big haulage of the Anasazi relics to Pueblo, Colorado. But the ranchers of Pueblo had had their fill of Indians too. The climate was wrong.

Next he tried what was then becoming the big town—Denver. There were civilized institutions there. One of them—the Colorado Historical Society—was interested enough to buy from him what he found.

Richard Wetherill at first called these people "the basket people," but moved on to calling them the Cliff Dwellers and then—probably helped out by the Indians who were good friends of his father—the Anasazi.

THE LAST winter I went there, the road to Spruce Tree House, Square Tower House, and the Sun Temple on Chapin Mesa were open. To get a view of Cliff Palace, Balcony House, and Sunset House however, I had to ski in. There is a logbook at the start of the trail in which you enter your name and the date and the time of departure. And then you are off, down a road surrounded with land which was farmed for the nine hundred or so years up to 1300, which has been terraced and check-dammed, down which for that near-millenium you would not have been able to progress without hearing the cries of Anasazi farm workers, the sound of fluters and singers.

It is a seven mile loop, and it is not hard going. But I found it psychologically hard. I was alone—my wife and daughter had decided to shop in snow-starved Durango. There is something strange in the way the olive green junipers and piñon pines may open up at any moment and give you a view southward or westward into an immense canyon, deep as Dante's inferno.

I told myself, "Just as far as Cliff Palace, and then you can turn round." Then of course, I changed my interior message to, "Just as far as Sunset House;" then to, "If you ski for another forty-five minutes you'll be at Balcony House, and then you'll be placed to finish the whole circuit."

From beautiful Cliff Palace, at which you can take off your skis and descend to the pueblo on its ledge below, you can see across Fewkes Canyon to Sun Temple. This is a great stone structure on the surface of the mesa, and for three or four generations, the families who lived at Cliff House would not have been out of sight of it. It was a communal ceremonial place for all the inhabitants of Chapin Mesa. It too, like the towers of Hovenweep, was built to be a solstice sun trap.

The great question which, according to the literature, perplexes the expert as much as the ordinary visitor is why the Anasazi left this area toward 1299, the beginning-of-the-exodus year for the Mesa Verdeans. The scholars say there are no simple explanations. The two times I have been there, I have been puzzled by the fact that the world of Mesa Verde is so much more desirable—so much more graced with complicated vistas and verdure—than the arid mesas on which the Hopi live, than the Zuni plateau in New Mexico, than most of the terrain of New Mexico or northeast Arizona where the Mesa Verdeans' descendants live. The climate is more desirable too—high and dry, and without the summer extreme you find in the areas occupied by the Hopi, Zuni, and Pueblo.

•

THE PLACE WHERE SOULS ARE BORN

In *Exploration: the Annual Bulletin of the School of American Research*, a copy of which I bought from a Navajo woman at the Mesa Verde bookshop, an archaeologist named Arthur Rohn suggests that the reason the Mesa Verde and Montezuma Valley people left had to do in part with a sort of philosophical or ideological wariness. As I mentioned earlier, there was a town of two-and-a-half thousand in the Montezuma valley. The idea of developing larger towns than already existed, that temptation to go metropolitan, would have meant an end to the egalitarian social arrangement which seems to have prevailed in the life of Mesa Verde and of such Montezuma Valley settlements as Yellow Jacket. The democratic Anasazi certainly had spiritual elites, but to quote Dr. Rohn, "to have developed beyond their thirteenth century achievements, they would have had to form social classes, develop craft specialties, and recognize an elite ruling class." That is, it is as if they had been taken to the mountaintop (where in any case they already lived) and been shown the towns of the plain, the chance to be Chicago or Manhattan or Paris, and had then refused to take that option.

What a startling idea! The Anasazi saints. Pre-Mormoning the Mormons!

In any case they began to move away. Perhaps not in a mass, perhaps more in the way Pueblo people have moved from place to place in historic times, clan by clan, family by family, faction by faction.

A fashionable theory just going out of favor when I first went to Mesa Verde was that drought had primarily caused them to move out. The drought idea got its large boost in the 1920s when A.E. Douglass developed his

•

system of tree-ring dating. All rings found in ancient trees in the region indicate there certainly was a drought between 1276 and the end of the thirteenth century.

But I wondered even then, if they moved out in time of drought, why in God's name would they go to the Hopi mesas or places of low rainfall like Zuni and Acoma in New Mexico?

A S I mentioned earlier, it used to be fashionable also to say that the Athabascan people, the Navajo and Ute and Apache, drove them out. But the Athabascan lacked horses in 1300. In all the cliff dwellings of Mesa Verde, there are only a limited number of routes to the farms on the mesa tops. Even if the stairs which the park service have since put in had existed then, a determined community could stave off any amount of assault.

One scholar, Linda S. Cordell, writes that the idea of the Anasazi as threatened by the Athabascan arises "when the United States was just about to enter a war, or was fighting one. The aggression model seems to tell us more about ourselves than about the Anasazi." When people talk about the Athabascan, again they think of John Wayne and Randolph Scott and wagon trains and Apache war parties on horseback. This image bears little relation to the first scattered family groups of Athabascan people who were just starting to arrive in the Southwest at the time of the Anasazi migration and who would have been a very poor threat to the clever folk of Mesa Verde.

Sensible scholars—of the kind fascinated laymen like me read in motels during blizzards—now say that the migration was complicated and gradual, though powerful

•

motives lay behind it. Again they look to the movements
of modern Pueblo and Hopi for a clue to what might
have happened on Mesa Verde and along the plush Montezuma Valley at the end of the thirteenth century. Hopi
towns and communities split up for theological and ceremonial reasons. Sometimes the splitting off has been
caused purely by the presence of European Americans.
The Mennonite missionary H.R. Voth and the perhaps
naively open-hearted Hopi leader Lololma caused such
dissension that early this century there was a movement
of Hopi away from Third Mesa to the lowland settlement
now called New Oraibi. The settlement of Hotevilla also
resulted from a split amongst Hopi over Voth and the
Mennonite faith. These were considered by the Hopi as
movements of awesome significance.

There was no European-American presence to acti-
vate the Anasazi departure, but just the same, doctrinal,
prophetic, factional reasons may have instigated it, and
once it began, perhaps the others followed out of a fear
of being left to die out on the mesa.

The kivas were—and in Hopiland and New Mexico
still are—subterranean lodge houses, a lodge being based
on ritual to do with a particular animal or vegetable species: corn, coyote, crow, eagle, jack rabbit. Descent into
them is through a central hole in the roof. I remember
how one steely February Saturday afternoon in the Hopi
First Mesa town of Walpi a number of pubescent boys
and girls descended into a kiva, carrying each a corn cob,
watched by an enormous gathering of Hopi Indians. The
children were eventually to emerge symbolically trans-
formed into lodge men and women.

At one stage a Hopi elder wearing feathers and an
off-the-shoulder, Buddhist-looking vestment ascended the

•

ladder, accompanied by an acolyte in a Bruce Springsteen American tour T-shirt. This had been a day when kachinas had come dancing and running on Third Mesa, a day when the sun had reached its late winter notch in the facing range to the south, the notch which portended the sprouting of beans in the warm kivas.

In the kiva, as it has always existed, are stone benches around the wall, a fireplace and a draft-deflecting stone which probably also has theological meaning, and above all a crease called the *sipapu* in the floor. This is the Place of Emergence, the notch through which souls enter the visible universe, climbing out of the mothering earth by way of the kiva's ladder and so entering the surface life of the world. In the Hopi and Pueblo world scheme, life comes only through the *sipapu* and *sipapuni* of the kivas of the Southwest. The *sipapu* is therefore the earth's vagina, the place where souls are born, each one in the lodge appropriate to its clan and its totem. Through the *sipapu* and up the ladder climbs all the energy and ambiguity of humankind.

I love big cities as much as any other urban decadent, and would find it hard to imagine life without the urban tumult and smell of spiritual and footpad danger. Just the same it has to be said that in big cities there are no *sipapu*. Mother becomes Ma becomes Mom. The city separates its citizens from the necessity of believing earth to be the chief of mothers. There are so many diverse trades in the big town, and it is from these, from the interaction between them, from the traffic of intentions rather than from the phases of the earth, that all plenty and all birth seems to derive.

The Pueblo Indians, living on barren ground in communities whose size might have been conditioned sublim-

•

inally by the decision of their ancestors the Anasazi to move out from Mesa Verde, are—again, without being sentimental about them—taken with the motherhood of earth. Hence the renowned Tewa Hopi song:

Oh our Mother the Earth, oh our Father the Sky,
Your children are we, and with tired backs
We bring you the gifts that you love. . . .

Did the Anasazi have their prophet Moses or Brigham, who urged them to move out from the more plentiful but more spiritually perilous life of the Montezuma Valley and Mesa Verde into desert ground, where the scantier essentials would not be such a source of spiritual confusion?

SEVEN

The Mile-High North America

HE MEN who were the first Europeans to encounter the Grand Canyon were disappointed
for two reasons. Members of Coronado's Monty
Pythonesque incursion into New Mexico in 1540, they
were looking for water and were disgruntled by the fact
that it was a perilous mile beneath the lip of the canyon
to get any. They were looking too for a good water route
to the golden Seven Cities of Cíbola, which didn't exist,
at least in a golden condition, but which they believed in
with a furious fixity.

John Wesley Powell, a one-armed rafter, came down
here in 1869 and honored the canyon for itself, arguing
in his journal that there would be disputes over water
rights and that these should be settled early and wisely
for the future sanity of the region. He seems to have been
an estimable man, this Civil War veteran. Every summer
Earl Kingston, husband of Maxine Hong Kingston, the

•

writer, comes to the canyon and stages a popular one-
man show based on Powell's life on the Colorado, and
though I've never seen it, I have at least dipped into
Powell's brave, sober journal and have heard Earl express
his frank admiration for the man. Powell was the first
European rafter on the Colorado and all its tributaries.
By the time he'd reached what is now the main tourist
section of the canyon, he had lived through the Canyonlands rapids, close to where the Green runs into the Colorado, where the river dropped thirty feet in a mile.

It is time for a confession, based on a knowledge
that you cannot fake places you haven't been. I have visited the Grand Canyon twice and neither time got to the
bottom of the Bright Angel Trail. I've never therefore
seen Phantom Ranch nor looked up at the intimidating
cliffs from Powell's point of view. The first time I was
there my daughters were under twelve, so we could not
sign on for the mule trip to the bottom nor could we
have left them while we hiked there and back.

This time, since it had snowed in the Grand Canyon,
and the Grand Canyon is never grander than under snow,
with the buttes frosted, with the mesquite, acacia and
tamarisk holding salient lumps with it, I skied some of
the way down the snow-covered Bright Angel. But the
short winter's day came toward a close, and discretion—
which as you know by now runs very high in my blood—
told me to return.

And so if you speak to me, you speak to a rimmer
not to a rafter.

In all my career as a writer going with mixed success
to New York to meet publishers, it was always the one
natural geographic item to which the pilot of whatever
plane—Eastern, American, United, Pan Am—would call

•

the passengers' attention. "Folks," the announcement would come from the cockpit, in a mellow voice which suited the mellow mood of a planeful of folk with the first cocktail of the day ingested already, "on the left of the aircraft, you can see the Grand Canyon . . ." The Missouri and Mississippi could be traversed without comment. But the great gulf of the Colorado made its claim on the attentions of pilots and travelers six miles up.

I'd also read that the Havasupai Indians had a lodge at the bottom of Havasu Canyon, one of the side canyons of the Grand, at a place called Supai, and that reservations were required if you were to go down there. The Havasupai have been in this stretch of the Grand Canyon since the 1100s or earlier. They are industrious farmers, following the same sort of *rancheria* or seasonal farm method of survival which the Papago and the Pima followed further south, around Phoenix and Tucson. They are related to various other tribes in whose name the word *Pai*—People—occurs: Havasupai, Hualapai (near present day Kingman, Arizona), Yavapai (people of the Sun, to the south of that but north of the Gila River). I had a telephone number which was supposed to allow one to make arrangements to stay at Supai, in the Havasupai's segment of the Grand Canyon. My wife and daughter and I had plans that we would ski down. Again, sadly, and as a price for having outlaid merely average as distinct from truly obsessed application to the project, we failed; the number I had for Supai never answered. In the hope of getting some information about all this from the Hualapai, relatives of the Havasupai, we took the loops up through Hackberry and Valentine, a lonely track amongst hilly, snow-drifted cattle country. It is wonderful western country, the Music Mountains to one

•

side of the road, the Cottonwoods to the south. But the Hualapai office in Valentine was shut. To take the road from Peach Springs into the Hualapai reservation was not permitted without prior arrangement.

A little about this loop before I get on with the confessions: A disused railway line follows the road. It was built in the nineteenth century to bring people into the Grand Canyon Caverns. The town attached to this tourist attraction has withered and is to a large extent boarded up. And it struck me that people aren't enthusiastic about caves anymore, the way nineteenth and early twentieth century people were. What is it about post-1950 people which has given to cave attractions everywhere this look of desuetude. Why has our sense of wonderment passed on, and what has it passed to? Why did honeymooners who went to the Grand Canyon in 1921 find it *de rigeur* to come up here by rail to the caverns as well, and why does no one think like that anymore? For the sidings and depots are shut, and the little towns of Hyde Park and Grand Canyon Caverns can barely keep their place on the map.

But again to the coming-clean. I have skiied to a distant view of the North Rim and have driven—against all the spiritual counsels of Edward Abbey—to a proximate view from its South Rim. But I do not know the whole story. I have not seen the canyon globally. This is the sin at the core of my story. I hope that so far along it will be overlooked.

THE COLORADO River comes down from what is now Utah and is dammed just south of the Utah–Arizona border at the town of Page, Arizona. Despite the dam though, the Colorado is still gouging into its socket—you are told the river carries away a half a million tons of sediment a day. It uses water-driven sand and gravel to gouge deeper still. Coming to startling Yavapai Point on the South Rim, looking over to the North Rim across the profound trench, you need no geology at all to understand that the Colorado has torn away and revealed here the red-orange, golden layers of the earth's age. The canyon's main walls are so clearly stratified in brown, orange-brown, tan, green-brown, umber, ochre, tan again. And the buttes and towers of rock, all layered in the canyon's robust colors, rise up in the enormous chasm. They have those irksome names: Diana Temple, Isis Temple, Tower of Ra, Osiris Temple, Zoroasta Temple, Wotan's Throne, Solomon Temple, Venus Temple, Jupiter Temple, Temple Butte, Sigfried Pyre, etc. etc. But they too bare their layers so graphically.

This is one of the first things you are told here: Rock layers near the top of the canyon and the buttes are about 200 million years old, but the rock right at the bottom of the gorge is 4 billion years of age. There are, to confuse the matter, the occasional volcanic rocks that are very recent—perhaps a thousand years of age. And not only did the river cut downward, but the rims also were thrust up by volcanic and other means. It is also noticeable to the layman that looking across to the North Rim, from some lookouts eighteen miles across, you are aware that the surface over there is much higher than the rim you're standing on. And so it is—twelve hundred or more feet higher than at Yavapai Point on the south side.

If there were not already sufficient awe, they tell you that there are six North American climate zones from the top of the mile-deep canyon to its bottom. Down at Phan-

•

tom Ranch, it is Mexico. Up here on the rim, especially of course on the North Rim, it is Canada. In between are represented the climates of Florida and the South, of the Midwest, of the Great Lakes, and so on.

Then the fossils: At various layers, seashells—for some of the layers were once ocean bed—dinosaurs, elephants, and camels can all be found fossilized here.

The dumb lay traveler drives into Yavapai Point on the Arizona 64, going west then via Hopi Point, Pima Point, and Hermit's Rest, doubles back then and runs past Grandview Point to Desert View, at which juncture the up-river Colorado veers away north toward the Painted Desert, the Navajo reservation, and Marble Canyon. It is apparent from all these vantages that the Colorado moves in extraordinary meanders. In the fifty-six miles of the South Rim available to the motorist, the river at the base of the canyon meanders for nearly 110 miles. Further to the west too it will make enormous bows and deviations, taking a detour northward for a long time before heading south, yet again passing Havasu Canyon, and reaching Lake Mead and the mud-gray canyons around Hoover Dam, over near Nevada.

Anasazi lived here on the South Rim at Tusayan. Here too are the sorts of astronomic buildings one meets at Hovenweep and at Sun Temple on Mesa Verde. Energetic farming was done here—the terraces and check dams can be seen. Just the same, this site doesn't overpower the imagination in the way Mesa Verde does. You get a sense that people didn't live quite as well here. You are aware too, as the country becomes barer to the east, along the route these people followed to the Hopi mesas in the great Anasazi exodus, that it would have been a testing migration, like that of the Israelites in Sinai, to

•

travel through the Painted Desert and over the Moenkopi Plateau, the area now known as the Navajo Nation.

At Moran Point, on the beautiful rim road, the reality of life on the canyon rim asserted itself. A herd of winter-famished deer were feeding off the lower branches of ponderosa pine. There are not too many motorists in winter—ice intrudes onto the View Drive. But those of us who were there parked and tumbled from our vehicles, anxious to encounter beings for whom life on the canyon rim was not a matter of a day's oohing and aahing, but a matter of continued breathing. How Abbey would have flayed and mocked and censured us. "If you wanted contact with this rawness all along," he would have raged, "then burn your goddam cars!"

I have to say on balance that the fiercesome Abbey was right. The North Rim meant more for me, because I put more into it. Without overstating how much that was, I can at least say I sweated and shivered for it. Arrivals by vehicle are in a curious way cheap arrivals. In summer private cars aren't allowed on the West Rim Drive anyhow, but of course buses are provided instead.

Only for the aged and infirm should some sort of motorized journey around the rim be permitted. The rest of us should not be made—as the sometimes misanthropic Abbey demanded—to travel on our hands and knees, but mules or bikes or our own hiking boots should be the conveyance. In an inhuman landscape, travel at a human pace. That's Abbey's law, and I believe it to be a valid one.

TO THE east of the canyon, the Little Colorado River gorge forms the border of the beautiful Painted Desert. Under ramadas, or open-sided shelters, Navajo rugged up against the north wind wait to sell you things— rugs, turquoise jewelry, belts. Whether you take the road down to Flagstaff or northeast to Tuba City, a Navajo town named after a chief who became a Mormon, you encounter the Navajo trading posts.

In this barren northeast quarter of Arizona, and spilling over into New Mexico and Utah, it is all Navajo country. This is the country from which the Navajo were for a period expelled by Kit Carson's army. From here they were coerced into their Long Walk to their concentration camp in New Mexico at Bosque Redondo. Those who wouldn't go were slaughtered in the bottom of Canyon de Chelly, amongst the Anasazi ruins there.

The Hopi Indian reservation lies right in the middle of the Navajo nation and is utterly surrounded by it. It has complicated and disputed boundaries with the Navajo. On the west and south the boundary is straight, but the northern and eastern borders feature a crazily snaking line. In the northeast, Navajo land forces a great peninsula into Hopi land. At Keams Canyon the two tribes share a hospital and other facilities. But they are passionately different people, and their emotions toward each other vary from a wary tolerance amongst moderates to outright contempt amongst conservatives.

The Navajo, as the Hopi will quickly tell you, took certain farming skills from observing the life of the Hopi pueblos. Appropriately, they farmed the old abandoned Anasazi fields in the rich bottom of Canyon de Chelly. They learned to weave at upright looms.

THE PLACE WHERE SOULS ARE BORN

As in aboriginal society, there were taboos against contact with mothers-in-law, and so the Navajo settled widely, living in round or hexagonal domed-shaped dwellings called hogans. You don't see so many hogans anymore. They're still in use in Monument Valley, but from Red Mesa and Mexican Water down through Kayenta, and from Tuba eastward into New Mexico, beyond Window Rock, the Navajo seem to occupy European-style housing. Perhaps many of them keep hogans somewhere, in less frequented localities. There has been, however, with an increase of population, great pressure on the land, and there are frequent disputes over grazing rights appearing before the Navajo grazing committees. The intensity of the pressure of increasing numbers of Navajo stock had led to the Bureau of Indian Affairs's edict that Navajo stock be compulsorily reduced. Though the tribal council thought there was some validity in the order, the great stock reduction of the 1930s and 1940s is still bitterly remembered. A Kayenta Navajo called Charlie Yellow recounts, "When they reduced the stock, many men, women, boys and girls died. They died of what we called ch'eena, which is sadness for something that will never come back . . ."

The head of the bureau at this stage was the poet John Collier, friend of D.H. Lawrence and Georgia O'Keeffe, a decent man heavily advised by bureaucrats. His name is accursed in the Navajo nation.

They say you are able to tell Navajo from Pueblo. Certainly the Navajo say you can. They consider themselves taller. Many Navajo men wear moustaches. Navajo women boast of small hands and long faces. Outsiders believe the Navajo look more Oriental than the Pueblo and Hopi. The back of their heads are, up to this point of history anyhow, flattened by the cradle boards on which the infants are toted about.

Much of their ritual is associated with sand paintings and with song, and the parallel with Central Australian aboriginal tribes is very strong.

"The young woman of the dusk," goes one of their translated Creation Myth chants,

> "May it be made as offering to her
> May it be made as offering to her;
> The pretty white shell,
> May it be made as offering to her,
> May it be made as offering to her . . .
> The pretty corn pollen,
> May it be made as offering to her;
> They will be exchanged for his voice, her mind;
> May they be made as offering to her;
> That which is good,
> May it be made as offering to her,
> May it be made as offering to her . . ."

There are a number of long and curative song ceremonials: the nine-day song cycle called the Mountain Topway; the *Yei Bichei*, or Nightway, where actors wearing masks representing Talking God, Water Sprinkler, Calling God, Fringe Mouth dance. Other "way" rituals meant to induce health, fertility, or to bring about marriages are called Blessingway; Shootingway is a ceremony to appease lightning; Beautyway appeases snakes.

THE PLACE WHERE SOULS ARE BORN

THE USE of peyote, the hallucinogenic cactus, reached the Navajo only when they were under great economic and spiritual threat, in the 1930s. Another endangered and disoriented group, the Ute, introduced them to the practice. A Road Chief of the Native American Church admits worshippers to the use of peyote during a dusk-to-dawn ceremony, which includes other officiants: Cedar Chief, Fire Chief. The peyote ceremonies occur particularly on the day before Thanksgiving, on Christmas Eve, the New Year, Easter, the Fourth of July, and Armed Forces Day. The reason the latter day has entered the Navajo Christian catalog of holy days is probably because the Navajo have served so bravely and in such numbers in the armed forces. (So, indeed, have the traditionally sedentary Pueblo and Hopi). The difference between the Navajo votary and the suburban hophead is that the use of the peyote to produce visions is authorized—and since 1960 in Arizona and 1956 in New Mexico—sanctioned by statute, but only in connection with church ceremonial.

In all native peoples under threat, similar vigorous but highly original versions, hybrids of Christianity and the old religion, emerge to help the people on their way. The Navajo have grown since the founding of the Native American Church. They are the largest tribal group. But they are also of course dispersed. They work in construction and heavy industry from New York to Los Angeles. Some return quite regularly to the Navajo nation, but if Navajo life—as is very likely, parallels Australian Aboriginal life—many probably stay away for good. For there are serious spiritual and ceremonial duties waiting for them at home, which they postpone. The longer they

•

155

postpone these duties, the less likely it becomes that they can face the elders again and confidently reclaim their part of the lodge ritual.

BLACK MESA and its three finger mesas, First, Second, and Third, are *Tuuwanasavi*, the Sacred Circle of the Hopi cosmology. From them you can see, looking south, the San Francisco Peaks where the kachinas live for the greater part of the year. To the south too is the White Cone system of buttes and mesas which are used as a means of reading the sun.

From First Mesa via Keams Canyon and Ganado runs an ancient road which always connected the Hopi with the Pueblo in New Mexico. This may be America's oldest thoroughfare, but these days it is called 264, and it takes you over Third and then Second Mesa and skirts the bottom of First before drawing you off to Window Rock and New Mexico.

Along this high, dry road in 1680 came Pueblo runners inviting Hopi to take part in the Pueblo uprising. The Hopi joined in energetically. At least four *Castilla* friars (the Hopi called all Spaniards *Castillas*) were killed. There would always be great resistance to the missionaries here, as with the Navajo also, whom the Hopi called the Head Pounders. The resistance to the Mennonite Voth, whose church was, much later, struck by lightning in 1942, was simply an afterword to the long rejection of the Franciscans.

When, after the Pueblo revolt, the missionaries ultimately returned about 1700, the town of Awatobi, the Place of the Bow, became a Christian village. A pause

•

was thereby brought to the essential Eagle Clan and Arrow Shaft ceremonies. Other Hopi in Oraibi, Walpi, Shungopovi, and Mishongnovi, so that they could take over the ceremonies and continue the cycle, decided that the population of Awatobi should be massacred. This massacre ultimately became a great source of shame to the Hopi, but behind it was their sense of the essential nature of Hopi ritual, its absolute necessity to produce the regular cycles of the known world.

People who felt this way were of course enthusiastic joiners in any attack on the *Castillas*. And even after the *Castillas* returned in 1693, the people of Walpi on First Mesa permitted the Pueblo from the Rio Grande villages to settle in Hano on First Mesa, where their descendents still live.

Most of these towns have been continuous communities for a thousand years or more, continuous agglomerations of people of the same ceremonial clans. Around about the time of the return of the Spanish to the Rio Grande at the end of the seventeenth century, a number of the settlements which had been below the mesas moved on top for defense. One of these was Walpi, which now rides the very end of First Mesa. It is a large village with a complicated system of alleys. Its inhabitants inhabit their peninsula of impregnable rock with some *sang froid*, as if this were the normal condition of humanity. I wonder: Is it the Hopi and Pueblo capacity to negotiate canyon sides which makes them so employable in the construction industry in Los Angeles and elsewhere?

On Walpi we were invited into a Hopi home. The world of Black Mesa is a dusty one, but the place was scrupulously swept, its floor a little lower than the earth outside. There was a refrigerator. The table was set for

•

dinner, and there were placemats. I couldn't help noticing the apparent gulf in what we choose to call taste between the superb miniature kachinas which were for sale, carved by members of the family, and the tawdry, cartoonlike three pigs who adorned the placemats on the dinner table. There was also an ornamental wall clock which featured an enormous wedge-tailed eagle.

It developed however, after a little conversation, that the members of the family were members of the Pig clan. The father of the family was a member of the Eagle. No outside decoration was too crass, as long as it was totemically true, to be fitted into the system of the household.

Kachinas, men wearing the masks and imbued with the divinities they represented, had appeared in Walpi that day. Just walking about. In the cold February air, around the corner of a building, you saw a glimpse of the bare-chested gods wearing their armbands, masks, aprons. "Next week," said one of the young men in Walpi, "the dances start properly. They go on for a day and a half." At the idea of the nonstop dancing he would need to do, his face was—I use advisedly this verb—*suffused*. I had a sense that he was in receipt of returns not superior perhaps to the returns we get from our social rituals but at least just as intense as anything we ever experience. And what that return was, I knew I would never understand.

EIGHT

Pimeria Alta

F YOU can still bear it, there is a similar departure story to that of the Anasazi in the country south of the Grand Canyon, in the beautiful Oak Creek Canyon and Verde Valley, in which Sedona, a town which bills itself as a focus for writers and painters, is located.

Sedona is astounding red rock country, a kind of inverted mesa approached by down-winding, magnificent roads. It deserves some consideration in its own right, separated from the question of its pre-Columbian life, however rich that was.

Like the Navajo's Monument Valley, Sedona has been heavily used for the movies and for fiction. Hence it is part of the geography of everyone's imagination. Zane Grey's *The Call of the Canyon* is set here. Long before most of us visit it, we have seen this country rendered cinematographically. Cecil B. deMille—according

•

to a Sedona legend—meant to create a studio here early in the century. He had been sent out west in 1913 to make a film called *Squawman* for the Jessie L. Lasky Feature Play Company. But as the train pulled into Flagstaff with deMille and the technicians and actors aboard it, a frightful twenty-four hour snowstorm hit the region.

Any winter visitor to the Southwest is familiar with this phenomenon. Blizzards seem to strike with particular suddenness and ferocity in northern Arizona and New Mexico, with a frenzy in fact up to the level of the summer thunderstorms of the region. We were snowed in by one such storm at Williams, Arizona, south of the Grand Canyon. Blinded by snow, we pulled off the highway about four. By 5:30 Williams was so snowbound that no traffic could move, and my daughter and I had to ski up the road to buy food. For Australians, it is a remarkable novelty to ski to the supermarket, to ski home with laden plastic bags in our mitts.

Anyhow, when deMille saw the intensity of the 1913 storm, he moved on to a more desert place. Sedona was saved for other artists.

Just the same all the best cowboys and cowgirls found occasional employment in Sedona. The local roll of honor includes Macdonald Carey, Robert Mitchum, Gene Autry—for some reason I can't now recall, an idol of my childhood. Glenn Ford worked here, Rock Hudson, the immortal Randolph Scott, evil Zachary Scott, Yvonne De Carlo, Henry Fonda, and Chill Wills. Even Elvis Presley in a movie called *Stay Away Joe*. Then *Broken Arrow*, that outrageous sentimentalization and diminution of the Apache; a fascinating Western just the same. Jimmy Stewart and Jeff Chandler and Debra Paget found employment in Sedona, together with William Holden and

•

THE PLACE WHERE SOULS ARE BORN

Ryan O'Neal and Rhonda Fleming and Robert Young, Cornel Wilde and Lizabeth Scott, Maureen O'Hara, Ray Milland, Dick Powell, Tyrone Power, Robert De Niro!

Europeans have always wanted to live in Sedona. The poor nomadic Yavapai who were found there once the Spaniards and the Yankees arrived were quickly did-dled out of their land, even out of their little farms, which lay around that classic open-plan (unwalled) western fort, Camp Verde. (The troops depended on the openness of the valley and on sentries for protection.) By contrast with the sadness of the Yavapai, no one is really tempted to diddle the Hopi out of their beloved but—to the Euro-pean sensibility—barren mesas.

General Crook and his troops would drive the Apache out of the area, and the place-names of the region seem to bespeak the methods. Bloody Basin, Skeleton Cave—scene of a massacre of Apache—Soldier's Pass and Soldier's Wash.

Some urbane people took the Apache's place. As one of Sedona's guidebooks says, it encourages "the artistic vision whether from the great or the weekend dabbler." One more-than-weekend dabbler who lived here, courtesy of the European upheaval which drove him out of Europe to America, where Peggy Guggenheim became his patron, was Max Ernst. In 1985 I was fortunate enough to stum-ble into a wonderful exhibition of Ernst's paintings and art in the Guggenheim Museum on Fifth Avenue. You went to the top level by elevator and encountered there the young Ernst of the Bauhaus and then wound down the Guggenheim's sublime spiral through Ernst's succes-sive decades.

He came to Sedona just after the end of World War II with his beautiful Californian wife, Dorathea Tanning,

•

and lived in Brewer Road, Sedona, till 1953. He created here his sculpture Capricorn, which in all consciousness seem to borrow from the red, God-struck escarpments all about.

BUT BACK to the central story. This area was occupied too by an Anasazi-style people who did not leave the Sedona, Oak Creek Canyon area till about 1400. A hundred and fifty years later, the Spaniards, seeing the towers and cliff dwellings these folk left behind, the ruins of Montezuma Castle, Tuzigoot, Honanki, and Palatki, named the departed inhabitants the Sinagua, the people who had lived without water.

Despite the Eurocentric names the Spanish applied to the remains they found, the Verde Valley and Sedona are lush and well-watered by comparison with the Hopi country. Yet the Sinagua—the ancestors of some of the Hopi—left the Verde Valley and Oak Creek Canyon to travel up through the desolation northeast of today's Flagstaff and to beg admittance to the Hopi mesas, leaving the area to the nomadic Apache and the Yavapai.

So why did the Sinagua, like the Anasazi, leave fine country and travel great, dry distances? This is exactly the sort of question that gives the Southwest a dimension Southern California does not have. In Southern California history is who won Best Supporting Actress in 1959. In places like Sedona, the questions of human evanescence, of the limits of what industriousness can achieve in a landscape, and of whether one needs to go into places of desolation to rescue one's soul are all less easily hedged.

There are what seem to be memories on the Hopi mesas themselves of the Sinaguan migration from sweet Sedona, or Palatkwapi, to the less plush life of the Hopi country. The clans called Raincloud, Water, Young Corn, and Rabbit Brush arrived at Walpi, a Hopi town built beneath a narrow prong of First Mesa, and applied for entry to the chief of the Snake Clan, which already lived there. The Sinaguan chief of the Water Clan—according to the legend—proved the suitability for the admission of his people by singing up a thunderstorm. He had done it before, and the myth looks after the question of why these people from Sedona were anxious to be admitted to First Mesa. In the plush world of the Verde Valley— so the oral history goes—they had become decadent and had been chastened with a great flood!

Another argument: in the plentiful Sinaguan rock peckings around Sedona, there are supposedly subtle signs—this to quote another ethnographer than Rohn, Linda Cordell—that a political elite was developing there, and such elites formed the basis for the growth from clan settlement to municipality. So there is the possibility that institutionalized inequality may have been behind the abandonment of Sedona, just as in Mesa Verde.

I F YOU should become an aficionado of the Sinagua and the Anasazi, the Four Corners region is crowded with their remains. North of Interstate 40, in Navajo country, there are the cliff dwellings of Kayenta and Keet Seel and Betatakin, and as if to prove Edward Abbey's view that the act of walking and stumbling is the only humane and humbling exercise which will prepare you for a sight of these places, all these need to be walked into.

Then there are the particularly fine ruins around Wupatki, on the cinder flows of Sunset Crater, northeast of Flagstaff. Sunset Crater itself is a continuation of the San Francisco Peaks. They are twelve thousand feet high but were sixteen thousand feet until the day in 1065 when the mountain system exploded. The earth near Sunset Crater was covered with cinders and ash, and water percolated through the ash layers and was retained there, safe from evaporation.

Wupatki is a beautiful Sinaguan pueblo on the cinder grounds. It stands amongst the lava flows and cones of iron oxide. Wupatki and the other nearby ruins show signs both of Aztec influence from the south and Anasazi influence from the north. It is believed some Anasazi from Kayenta, up near the Grand Canyon, moved into this area at the same time as the Sinagua and lived in a neighborly manner with them.

Wupatki is a fine masonry condominium on a red spur of volcanic soil. It was one of a number of towns in the region exploiting the new conditions following the volcanic explosion in the eleventh century. There's a wonderful amphitheater here, like a large open air kiva, I suppose, and most noticeable of all, a ball court, where the Sinagua played a ball game which had religious significance—though of course in Wupatki, religion *was* sport, art, theater. Even the peeling of a yucca pod for domestic purposes had its religious meaning.

The game played in Wupatki's arena is supposed to have been like the ball game of the Aztecs and probably came here by way of the Sonoran Desert in Mexico. Two bands of young men competed for possession of a ball which must be tossed, carried, and worked toward a ring affixed to the wall of the court and then dropped through. One wonders what enthusiasms and nuances of rules attended this contest. There were totem animals associated with each team which contended on this court in the twelfth century. Our association of teams with particular totems is a profound tendency, even if we would like, as if to distance ourselves from the players of Wupatki, to pretend that these days it's all merely p.r. cuteness.

At Wupatki too the remains of macaws and parrots have been found—another sign of traffic with Mexico.

Wupatki was abandoned about forty years before the Mesa Verde people left their homes. There are signs that drought had its effect here too, but the reasons for the evacuation are again uncertain. The idea that certain social and religious perceptions may have spread like a virus through the Southwest from settlement to settlement and caused some sort of fashion for emigration naturally tickles the mind.

I NOTICED that with the Hopi and the Pueblo running has always been an ardent sport, a religious matter, and a means of communication. At Taos pueblo, for example, there is an east–west footrace track between the two halves of the pueblo. A Californian named Peter Nabokov has written a fascinating treatise on the religious-cum-contemplative-cum-sporting dimensions of what he calls "Indian running." The universal Indian practice of

•

167

ritual athletics, both in individual and relay form, created astounding Jim Thorpe, and the Hopi champion Louis Tewanima.

. The greatly successful Pueblo uprising against the Spanish in New Mexico in 1680 was organized and coordinated, pueblo-to-pueblo, by Indian runners. Word was got even to the Hopi mesas in Arizona, and in 1980 the uprising run was reenacted. It took five days in 1680 and in 1980 for Pueblo Indian runners to get from Taos, down the string of Rio Grande pueblos as far as Santo Dominingo, then northwest through Jemez and on to Acoma and Zuni and finally to the Hopi towns.

I began to wonder if perhaps the idea of moving out of Mesa Verde and Hovenweep and the Sedona/Verde Valley region was spread pueblo-to-pueblo in the thirteenth century by the same means.

In any case, whatever caused these great thirteenth and fourteenth century goings-forth, the people of the Anasazi exodus did not seek to move too far away from the mountains. The Hopi pueblos, east of Tuba City, look out at the San Francisco Peaks. The Pueblo and Zuni of New Mexico can see the San Juan, the beautiful and close by Sangre de Cristos. Mountains figure large in the cosmology of all three related groups.

THERE IS a great massif which runs to the south of Hopi/Anasazi country—America's tallest east–west running range. The part of it called the Mogollon Rim runs two hundred miles across eastern and central Arizona. It is the great divider in Arizona, a frontier between two distinct realities. South of the Rim, the Sonoran Desert begins. Whether you leave southward from Camp Verde or head off the rim from the scenic towns of Payson or Show Low, you are soon aware, even in the mountains on the way to Phoenix, that the world is changing.

It is here, south of the great Mogollon Rim and the Gila River, that European America has made its two largest Arizonan cities—Phoenix and Tucson. Prophets like the late Edward Abbey and the writer Chuck Howard say these communities cannot last, that the same realities of climate and rainfall which have always governed the lives of the Sonoran Desert Indians called the Papago and the Pima will in the end catch up with sun-crazed Phoenix and Tucson.

The facts of the area, says Chuck Howard, are that precipitation ranges between three and twelve inches a year, and evaporation ranges from six to nine feet. The imbalance cannot be altered by technology. So that is that. The equation is impossible.

You can feel the brash tenuousness of Phoenix and the vaunted and booming Valley of the Sun to the east. And the tenuousness of sprawling Tucson as well. Someone remarked that it took Phoenix 105 years from its Yankee founding in 1860 to found a historical society; it was as if people took that long to become convinced that the city's license might not at any second be canceled by the realities of the Sonora.

The city was named Phoenix because one of its first settlers thought that it would rise phoenixlike from the Hohokam ruins on the proposed town site. Phoenix turned out in the short term to be a wonderfully apposite name for the place, in the sense that its population grew five times over between the end of World War II, when it was only fifty thousand, and the year 1960. Like Tuc-

•

son and Albuquerque, it has burgeoned with a startling recklessness to provide its quintupling population with ranch houses and gardens and swimming pools.

Now Phoenix is well over a million people. And what a spread it is to travel through, west to east. Scottsdale, Tempe, Mesa, Chandler, Gilbert, Paradise Valley, Glendale and Sun City all hugely sprawl to the east. It is as long, and just about as banal, to drive west to east across Phoenix as it is to drive south to north across the much more densely populated Los Angeles.

TUCSON WAS a Spanish mission and then military settlement—the presidio of San Augustin—but it too grew from a few thousand in 1945 to about three quarters of a million now. It is a significant city in the dispensations of earth: It is the largest settlement on earth whose water supply comes entirely from groundwater, or to use Chuck Howard's term, "fossil water," pumped water from beneath the earth.

Then, eastward in arid New Mexico, Albuquerque was a 1706 offshoot from the Spanish town of Santa Fe. And again, it was a modest establishment until the Manhattan Project and other startling human technological adventures blew its city boundaries wide. Like Tucson, it went through its stages as Spanish presidio, garrison town, modest commercial center, Yankee railway town, and then groundwater boomtown.

All three towns boast in all their civic literature and on as many billboards as they can manage about their yearly percentage of sunshine—in Tucson it is said to be over three hundred and fifty days in the year, that is, over

•

ninety percent of the year. This—say the Arizonans— makes Miami's sixty-two percent a despicable figure. But of course, the prophets warn these figures do not ultimately demonstrate the desirability of these Sonoran towns. They demonstrate their lack of viability.

In Australia there is no rush to the interior, to towns with similar rainfall and climate to that of America's three great desert cities. That is probably because the coasts of Australia are temperate. Perhaps to have cities of such dramatic demographics as these three, you need the great, snow-bound and ice-blasted cities of the northeast, a great pool of aging men and women who do not want to shovel snow or risk the femur-cracking ice pavements of Chicago and New York.

But, oh, the ugliness of the commercial strips, the endlessness of the car lots in all three cities, the repetitions of trailer home parks where America's once frostbitten aged come to grow their melanomas during the relentlessly sun-blasted days.

What these three great desert towns needed to achieve their present suspicious size was an indulgent federal government, willing to locate its bureaus and instrumentalities in these unlikely places; willing to place defense and research establishments in their hinterlands. Willing above all to subsidize the expense of the pumping and desalinization of water, the expense of channeling electricity from distant places. Chuck Howard sees Tucson as an athletic youth pumped full of anabolic steroids by an indulgent federalism. Its short-term performance will be startling, but its ultimate destiny will be seizure.

These are remarkable human constructs in any case, anomalies of history, the only great cities of history to have existed in places so lacking in cloud.

•

In some ways Phoenix and Tucson and Albuquerque, particularly the latter two, are superb. Anyone who can afford a middle-class house gets a villa of great convenience, air-conditioned and long-eaved. The gracious eye of Frank Lloyd Wright, mediated down to other Southwestern architects, is visible in the design. Fossil water sits in the blue backyard swimming pools, indifferent for the moment to the sun's heroic evaporation. The *good* suburbs are very civilized. A middle-class home in Albuquerque, Tucson, or Phoenix will have much finer artwork than anything you're likely to find in a Philadelphia suburb. There will be Navajo rugs, Santa Fe paintings, Pueblo pots, Hopi kachinas. There may be fragments of Anasazi pottery as well, the beautiful black-on-white.

All the marks of civic culture are present. In Albuquerque, for example, there is the Indian Pueblo Cultural Center, the Albuquerque Museum, the New Mexico Museum of Natural History. There are craft galleries. There is a Fine Arts Center at the university where opera and symphony concerts are held. At Christmas thousands of people, most of them first-generation citizens of the city, make their commitment to the traditions of the place by constructing traditional *luminarias*, brown paper bags ballasted with sand in the bottom and containing a candle, which pick out the contours of roofs and gardens in a way which the locals say is quite charming.

In summer in Santa Fe, north of Albuquerque, the opera is to be attended, open air, in the hills a little to the north of the city. The Albuquerquean is often lean and aerobically fit and can raft, swim, or paddle a canoe down the Rio Grande rapids, or cross-country ski in the Sangre de Cristos.

The Phoenix and Tucson people have the same enthusiasms, and Phoenix has the most sophisticated range of visible cultural tokens—the Phoenix Symphony, the much-praised Scottsdale Symphony, the Arizona Opera. In Scottsdale, Taliesin West is located, which since 1937 has been the winter base of some seventy architects, staff, and students of the Frank Lloyd Wright School of Architecture. There is an art museum and the great Heard Museum of Anthropology and Primitive Art. It's a delight to see exquisitely tanned young Arizona mothers and their bronzed, healthy children looking at the Heard's wonderful collection of quite astounding Hopi kachinas. Brisk, sun-primped mothers raising a race of swimming and tennis-playing *herrenvolk* where the icy winds never sear the flesh.

But beware, says the prophets! All this gloss is based on fossil water—in the argot of this day, a nonrenewable resource, a boon which brings with it to the surface salt in solution; salt, that old maker of desolations.

Eighteenth century Spanish missionaries, who in this part of the world were Jesuits in the days before the Spanish Emperor expelled the Jesuits from Spain and its dominions, passed judgment on the desert Papago for eating dead, diseased, and rotten carcasses. For treasuring an occasional feast of rat. But then the Jesuits had their wagon trains from Sonora province, Mexico. Today's wagon trains arrive in the cities of the desert in the form of voltage from other states, natural gas from Texas, and that good old fossil water from beneath the ground. As Chuck Howard says, "Days long past pour from their faucets, feed their families and power their worlds."

TO THE south of Tucson are all those remains of the Spanish religious and military empire. Of the former, the most superb is the mission of San Xavier del Bac, Father Kino S.J.'s mission to the Pima and Papago.

These tribes welcomed Jesuit missionaries to what Kino called their *rancherias*, or farms. For reasons of religion and perceived advantage, the Pima and Papago always welcomed the Jesuits, perhaps because they knew the protecting cavalry, in however small numbers, was never far behind them. Bac was a particularly promising place for the missionaries, in that it seemed to have had year-round water.

At Bac, Kino was the first European to find and record evidence that California wasn't its own island. In the eighteenth century, there was newspaper and scholarly discussion in favor of the idea that the enormous Gulf of California continued far north and made California a country of its own. Kino's conversations with the Indians at San Xavier del Bac in late April and early May 1700 showed that the blue abalone shells with which the Papago decorated themselves had been traded overland by Indians from the Californian coast.

This evidence would make a number of later journeys northwest to the Californian coast inevitable. It, for example, is the reason the landscape northward from Santa Fe, and into Utah and back to northern Arizona, is littered with the name of Escalante, or else with the Spanish names he applied to natural features.

The Indian rancheria of El Tusonimo—Tucson—became an outstation of San Xavier.

From the start, and under Jesuits and Franciscans, San Xavier del Bac was terrorized by the Apache, as were many fixed communities of Indians and Spaniards at this extremest limit of Spanishdom. There is a strange mixture of terror and graded prejudice in the account of a Franciscan friar named Maynard Geiger who visited from Santa Barbara, California, in 1802, and wrote the sort of things missionaries and others had been writing in New Mexico and Arizona since the first European contact. "The Apache Indians are mortal enemies not only of Christians but of everybody. They go about the whole area robbing and killing to get what they can. . . . Nor are the many presidios which are located here for that reason only of any avail to restrain them. For this reason the soldiers are organizing a campaign against them. . . . Not only the soldiers but the mission Indians in recent days, those of San Xavier and Tucson which is a *visita* from here, together with Papagos and Gilenos, went out against them. Though these latter are pagans, they realize that the Apache are their enemies."

"Though these latter are pagans . . ."

Maynard Geiger's dispatch is a minor but emblematic one from a war of attrition with the Apache, which would last just short of three hundred years.

I WENT down to the former garrison of Tubac with a descendant of eighteenth century Spanish settlers, a group who consider themselves rather separate from today's immigrants, and who are therefore a key to the complicated nature of Arizona society.

For Arizona, on the face of it, pretends to have no more history than the latest golf course or trailer park. But it is layered and affected by history and by gradations of race and class.

This man's family owned the old schoolhouse in Tubac, a town which is a modest tourist center now. Like the rest of Pimeria Alta, it became part of the United States not through General Stephen Kearny's great capture of Santa Fe in 1846 but as part of the Gadsden Purchase of 1853. For all families who—like my friend's—have been here so long, there are still memories of the Apache and of sundry glories and degradations. Tickle the old families of Tucson and you get a story of dogged brutality, dealt and received.

The old Arizonan pre-Gadsden families give lip service to the Yankee Protestant ethic, but there is also an ancient hidalgo pride barely submerged. They adjusted long ago to the Yankee acquisition of their region. It is still a live issue here just the same, even though it does not take an overt separatist direction. It burns away. Its voice is strong too in the barrios of Tucson amongst the more recent arrivals, in the suburbs to which the Yanqui Tucson people go slumming to drink mescal, listen to Mexican bands, and eat *real* Mexican food.

In any case, from Tubac, with which my friend's family had been long associated, from this tiny presidio and its scatter of barracks and chapel and blacksmith's shop, at a time in the eighteenth century when the eastern American states were straining toward the self-assertion which led to independence, came the impulse to colonize northern California.

A little sign in front of the Tubac schoolhouse says that in 1775 one Juan de Anza, the captain of the presidio, moved out of Tubac, with 240 colonists from the Mexican provinces of Sinaloa and Sonora and with a thousand head of livestock, to the Californian coast. They were making toward Monterrey, and they would be the originators of the mission and presidio of San Francisco.

Up until 1860, Tubac was one of the larger towns of Arizona, but the American Civil War stripped the area of the garrison that was needed to intimidate the Apache, and then the railway went to Tucson, that old *visita* of the San Xavier mission, and worked its difference there.

MANY PEOPLE point to the heroic ancients of the Phoenix area, people called the Hohokam, as a picture of what might happen to Phoenix and other Sonoran and desert cities in the future. The very name Hohokam is claimed to be a clue. It is a Pima Indian word meaning "all used up."

The Hohokam were relatives of the Anasazi. In fact, over by the Roosevelt Lake area east of the city are the ruins of Indian pueblos which are believed to have been occupied by Anasazi and Hohokam and Mogollon people all living within the same broad community.

The Hohokam began farming in the Phoenix area fifteen hundred years ago, and they became extraordinary irrigators. Education systems, such as animated and still cartoons, have instilled into the popular imagination the belief that all good things began with the coming of the wheel. But the Hohokam, like the Celts thousands of miles away across the Atlantic, were a wheelless people. Their energy is all the more brave and touching, especially since it was expended in a landscape that pursued its own agenda of what would be tolerated.

So the Hohokam tapped the Gila, Salt, and Verde

Rivers for irrigation. The Hohokam canals, we are told, already connected the whole region about the time the Roman Empire was fragmenting. Running thirty feet wide and fifteen feet deep, they carried water to fields miles from the source.

In the 1860s, Anglo pioneers drew on the Hohokam system of canals which still mark the country around Phoenix, and the Pima Indians, who may have been descendants of the Hohokam but who restricted themselves to the seasonal (as distinct from permanent) fields and settlements called *rancherias*, have always used the residual complex of Hohokam canals where possible.

Irrigation, which made intensive farming possible for the Hohokam, liberated them to pursue the arts; particularly the art of etching designs by the use of acidic cactus juice into seashells acquired from the Gulf of California. But, again to quote the desert prophets Abbey and Howard, irrigation was overused, and Hohokam fields were frequently imperfectly drained. So the dissolved salts in the water were spread across the farmlands and remained on the earth when the water evaporated. The arable land died, and the highly settled nature of Hohokam life was rendered impossible.

The *rancheria* Pima and Papago are believed to be descendants of Hohokam who moved downstream, southward, looking for new land, their dispersion helped along by feuding and factionalism. The earth, it turned out, permitted only the *rancheria* style of life.

Many people in Phoenix, not just Chuck Howard, say that pattern is ineluctable, that we cannot do anything to make salt evaporate or alter the direction the rain comes from and in what quantity it falls. Arizonan farmers in the west of the state, over near fabled Yuma, have settled the problem of salinity for the moment by installing an expensive drainage system to take salt-laden water from their fields and into the Colorado River system. Carried south to Mexico, it has devastated farming land either side of the Colorado estuary. Some of the Mexicans flitting across the border—although *flit* is a whimsical word and hardly matches the evil reality of their passage to America—are fleeing farmland which has died of America's salt.

JUST TO the west of Tucson you encounter a system of life which makes brave deals with the desert and has better success than the Hohokam: The concentrations of giant saguaro cacti in the Saguaro National Monument. The great stands of saguaro always had a central and crucial part in the cycles and rituals of Sonora. They impress the visitor. I felt they had something of that mute but palpable tolerance you seem to get from other giants, the whale and the red kangaroo, say. The two sections of the national monument, east and west of the city, are like dormitory suburbs to the giant cactus, and to Tucsonians, so rich in food and water and fuel, they are for the moment merely a diversion. Most facile travelers like myself take a pleasant day's swing out through Old Tucson, the movie set town built for the film *Arizona* in 1940, a park a little B-grade in character—the sort of place which recurs a great deal in the less distinguished late night Westerns or in television repeats.

And then, after Old Tucson, we gawk our way through the saguaros and find that they are not B-grade at all. In late afternoon we emerge almost gratefully, released at last from awe, on the northwest edge of Tucson, within sight of good old Interstate 10. The reason for the awe is the size and spread and painstaking mechanisms of the saguaros. They are almost too much desert reality for the urban human to take in with comfort. That again, is the great feature of the Southwest. There are plenty of places you can go for a brief fright.

You can even savor in retrospect, the advice contained in the national monument's handout. "If a joint of cactus becomes embedded in your skin, try to flip it away by using two sticks or similar objects as levers." In that period when—beginning with *Jaws*—appalling films were made about rogue giant creatures imbued with a human malignity, the failure to exploit the saguaro is difficult to explain.

I think we recognize a kinship to the saguaro too, as the afternoon passes and we find out how a walk amongst them can dry out an organism even in winter and begin to wonder how they can maintain such height and permanence here. For the saguaros are like us, vertical columns of water in a dry place. Their life span is about two hundred years, and they live seventy-five years and to a height of twenty feet before they put forth their first branches. I became fascinated by the fact that all the great, fleshy, carapaced, and spined limbs develop from the same level of the main trunk, and in some big robust beasts of saguaros, a second inner series of branches develops from a point further up the trunk again, and all the branches in that series grow from the same exact level.

Six thousand feet above, up the slopes of the Rincon Mountains, there are Douglas fir and ponderosa pine— there is more rain up there. But down in the desert scrub,

the saguaros managed to achieve height only by producing themselves in this form, desert gothic, thick-skinned
and spiky. And within all is moisture.

In the gift shops at Old Tucson and at Tucson airport, you can buy cactus jelly, made from the fruit the
saguaro puts forth in spring. But given that Arizonan
society is so well supplied from other places, people don't
call much on the cactus. They grow mound cactuses and
ocotillo in their gardens—the ocotillo are the thin-branch
cactuses whose straight branches can be used to make
fences throughout the Sonoran region, and which are still
regularly used for the purpose in Pimeria Alta.

But basically, except in the scenic, gardening sense,
the cactus doesn't impinge on the lives of people in Phoenix or Tucson.

For the Indians the saguaros and other cacti were
obviously a whole economy of bounties. They were, for
a start, history. The Pima and Papago took wood from
the long ribs of the saguaro and carved an account of
what happened each year into it. The saguaro therefore
provided Papago memory on a stick; long streaks of history. These wooden ribs were also used for everything
from doors to bird cages.

You can see hard disks and pits of scar tissue on the
saguaro, caused by and then occupied by birds, and the
Papago used these as bowls.

Then when the fruit came out on the saguaro, it was
energetically harvested and gratefully devoured. The Papago
year began with this June harvest, when the saguaro were
fat with the stored moisture which would have to last them
until the monsoons arrived in autumn and winter.

The sugary, pulpy, seed-ridden saguaro fruit could
be eaten as it came off the tree or boiled or pressed so

•

that the juice could ferment. The seeds themselves could be pressed for oil or ground to make a flour. June was then, as the American idiom has it, *fat city*. In this same desert in which Tucson booms, the rest of the Indian year could be frightfully lean. I was fascinated to read about a Sonoran tribe, on the southern border of Arizona and over in northern Sonora, a tribe called the Seri, who needed to save their excrement so that undigested seeds could be extracted from it and reused for nutrition.

Harvesting of cactus fruit ended in a wine ceremony toward the close of June. The fermented saguaro juice was looked on as a beneficence. A fete of wildness began, and missionaries were affronted. But the purpose of all this cactus-juice license and orgy was to induce turbulence in the sky and produce rain.

Dizzy women
Are seizing my heart.
Westward they are leading me.
I like it.

We are told that women painted birds and butterflies on their breasts, and men painted the soles of their feet red, wanting them to glimmer in the firelight when at last the juice felled them.

Ready, friend!
Are we not here drinking?
The Shaman's drink
The magician's drink!
We mix it with our drunken tears and drink.

The orgiasts dreamed and went to the sky in their dreams, making a connection between the mute water the

•

cactus had pumped up out of the earth into its massive body and the pending, thunderous monsoonal water in the heavens.

To find such tribal and ritual precedents for getting tanked always appeals to a boozer, just as the tale of the use of peyote by Navajo mystics, relayed to the world in the works of the writer Castaneda, appealed to the hop-heads. But maybe Papago booze worked purely because it had a specific ritual and seasonal place. In demytholo-gized society, at the cocktail hours of Tucson and Phoenix, booze—disassociated from its seasonal prescriptions—is merely something to assuage the rigors of the day. For the Plains Indians and the Apache, it became a succulent, strange lunacy which, in disturbing times, as the aliens streamed in by wagon and train, bore the brain away. And for modern Papago, it has probably—in the form of Jim Beam and vodka—taken on that same disassociated meaning.

But cactus juice was in fact, like peyote, provided by divinities only so that humans could briefly explore the zone of stupefaction. In the drunken brain, the world is a level playing field. Miraculous events can happen there. Every boozer likes the suspicion that liquor is capable of calling up a higher reality. *In vino veritas*, we like to assure ourselves. But the truth of liquor may well be that perhaps we were never meant to have our brains leveled out in that way without the sort of divine sanction the Papago had at their rain festival and without the preced-ing disciplines of a year lived in the Sonora.

The saguaro, drawing up water into its fluted body, expands and contracts as it uses up its moisture, and the contraction itself cuts down on evaporation. We'll never see a finer adaptation to the desert than it is. The other

•

baroque plants of the desert, the cholla—the jumping cactus, which is suspected of actually leaping at the body—the agave, the ocotillo, each have similar means, produce their fruit in season, and last equally well. The Pima and the Papago had a sense that they themselves were minor, unrooted, and fragile desert actors by comparison.

And that perception is the correct one. Right across this band, from the Sacramento Mountains in New Mexico through the Sonora to the Mojave in California, despite the cities of fossilized moisture which litter the Southwest, despite the little amethyst reservoirs of moisture in which the surburbanites swim all year round, it is possible through a combination of bad luck—a breakdown on an unfrequented road, an inadequate supply of water in the cooler in the back seat—to perish very quickly, wandering, unrooted from the groundwater which the saguaros exploit.

The Sonoran towns of Arizona have this in common with the settlements of Central Australia. Everybody in both places has tales of terrible and swift "perishings" from lack of water, of the predeath craziness which unbalances the victim, of bloating and eventual mummification beneath the sun.

The first Europeans to perish here were forty-niners, on whom both thirst and the Apache made considerable inroads. The Apache proved to be an ultimately evanescent danger. They live now, coming to terms with the dominant culture, in their reservation at San Carlos. No brutal cavalry unit however can cow the sun. The three hundred and some days of unblinking light of which Phoenix boasts will have their way very rapidly with anyone who is suddenly alone in the scrub and who is foolish or unprepared.

•

THE PLACE WHERE SOULS ARE BORN

IN 1853 James Gadsden, the American minister to Mexico, made the final adjustment to the Mexican–American border by purchasing a swath of desert country which ran from the western borders of Texas to the Colorado River at Yuma. One of the motives was to provide ground on which a transcontinental railway could run. But the new border was a gratuitous one for the Pima, Papago, and Yuma. They all had relatives and dreams and rituals associated with Mexican places. The Papago, for example, used to show their daring by wading into the Gulf of California and letting the waves break across their chests. They were then required to run beside the sea twenty miles at a time and to bring back salt. Men died in an attempt to run themselves into a state of vision, break the wall, and get through to the contemplations beyond.

Indian borders were of course different from energetic Gadsden's, and they still exist and are even in their way recognized by mainstream America. West of Tucson, the Growler Mountains is one. Beyond them, the rainfall is low. This used to be the country of the group called the Sand Papago, who didn't live in *rancherias* of the kind in which Father Kino discovered the Papago of Bac. The Sand Papago traveled in very small clan groups, moving in established patterns, knowing their ground, knowing where the earth's scarce food and hidden water were, not lingering to become fat at one source.

Now these people are extinct.

It wasn't that anyone wanted their ground, which is made up of the Organ Pipe Cactus National Monument, a wildlife refuge, but above all, bombing and gunnery ranges and military proving grounds. It is just that their resources were so delicately balanced that American intrusion—along with all the normal moral and medical disasters which befell indigenes—meant death. They lived, when they lived, beyond the rainfall boundary, and that governed their life and made them vulnerable.

Yuma, over on the Colorado, and the little towns of Somerton, Gadsden, and San Luis average less than four inches of rain a year. They too boast at their town limit of unrelenting sunshine—ninety-three percent of their days go utterly unclouded! Sunshine isn't their problem. They live by cattle and by irrigation from the Colorado. And send their salt to Mexico.

The first time I ever saw Yuma it had that look Australian towns do when they're hanging on in a zone of dryness: the inevitable look of an oasis of convenience trying to be a terminus. Yuma has fifty thousand people, by grace of the Colorado. Nor is it distracted—as is Mesquite in the northeast of Nevada or Wendover in Utah— by the tarty, neon-winking of casinos beyond its border. Yuma has a kind of undistracted stillness but also an air of waiting for the 9:10 to roll out. It is not Phoenix or Tucson in any case. Even in the plentiful States, they could not get by on Yuma's limited rainfall.

FOR ALL those Mexicans who work in Tucson and Phoenix, who drive round those streets of supposed Yankeedom with their rear window carrying a transparent but heavily tinted transfer of Our Lady of Guadalupe, the main port of entry is Nogales. Nogales, Arizona, is not such a fancy town that you are drawn to reflect on its wealth in contrast with Nogales, State of Sonora, Republic of Mexico, which is a few yards away. Yet the contrast is there just the same. There are some superb villas in Nogales, Mexico, and a wonderful restaurant called La Rocha, which sits indeed on a cliff face above the railway line and which fashionable people drive all the way from Tucson to dine at.

But there are also hovels worthy of Baguio, the Philippines, or Khartoum, Republic of Sudan.

For most suburbanites in the developed world, it is a serious journey to go to the Third World, but citizens of Tucson can go there for the afternoon. From the world of the fixed retail price to that of barter, from welfare to beggary and the cunningly adjusted wit of skinny Mexican street vendors who know how to milk the *gringo*. An arch but accurate cry is heard in Nogales, Mexico, which is not heard in Nogales, Arizona. "What is an extra dollar to you, *señor?*"

Through Nogales, going north through the inspection booths where Mexico ends, come the girls taking the clever recipes up to Tucson, to cook in some barrio restaurant or middle-class home. Nogales, Mexico, is probably a wealthy Mexican city, living in brotherhood with Nogales, Arizona. But you return over the border at the end of the afternoon still with the question of this extraordinary juxtaposition, cornucopian America and cash-hungry Mexico, unexplained.

Further east, at the smelting town of Douglas, its sister town on the south side being Agua Prieta, the contrast seems greater. Agua Prieta is not set up for tourism. Douglas itself is a sprawling and rather melancholy mining town. But there's money there, even if Douglas has

•

some of that wide open, watchful, wistful, waiting look that Yuma—at the other corner of the state—has. Douglas has had a very quiet existence since Geronimo, the supreme figure of an irreducible Apache leader, surrendered there a century ago.

So Agua Prieta and Douglas aren't as symbiotic to each other as the two Nogales, *Ambos Nogales*, are. Look at Douglas and then at Agua Prieta and you encounter the great problems of writing about the American Southwest. Mexico impinges. Arizona and New Mexico are not sealed systems, one from the other. Mexico is the land from which the domestics, the cooking, and the cocaine comes. This land to which the outlaws were always fleeing in the cinemas of our childhoods, this land to which the salt travels and whose chief manufacture is the gardener and the maid.

The systems and jurisdictions don't cross the border, but reality and the hordes of legal and illegal immigrants do.

You encounter some astounding border phenomena as well. A little before I went through there, the Douglas–Agua Prieta border was the scene of an incident characteristic of the problems the Americans have with their long river-and-desert border with Mexico. A Mexican drug dealer living in Agua Prieta's last street before the border owned a house which was directly across from a cement business on International Street, the border thoroughfare in Douglas. He constructed a tunnel from one to the other. It was expertly built over six months, and the hydraulics, drainage, and excavation probably cost as much as $3 million.

In the drug dealer's house in Agua Prieta the entire

billiard table and the platform on which it stood could be lifted by hydraulic jacks concealed beneath the floor. Packages of cocaine could then be taken down to trolleys in the tunnel and wheeled beneath the border, beneath the drainage ditch on the American side, to a ladder which rose to a spacious chamber beneath a drainage cover in the cement plant. The purchase of this plant cost the dealer a further $2 million. Such are the resources of the drug smuggler.

The Agua Prieta tunnel and a number of related ones along the border probably cost at least $120 million to set up in all. The border patrol lacks such budgets.

The most horrifying aspect of this story is that the on-site drug dealer and his backers and associates from further south then had the twelve laborers who had worked on the tunnel shot and thrown into a pit near Douglas. In Tucson the five Mexican surveyors responsible for directing the tunnel accurately beneath the border were all shot dead too over a period of a day or so, before they could spend their accumulated wages on tequila and gifts to take home to their wives and children.

In New Mexico and Arizona, the desert and mountain border is immense and largely desolate. Officers of the border patrol cover it on horseback and in four-wheel drives whose best days are past. Smugglers, often in the illegal immigrant business as well, send their clients over with packages of narcotics for delivery on the other side—part payment for the clients' having been inserted into the United States. Drugs also come north in false compartments in the floors of vehicles, in specially adjusted gas tanks, in souvenirs, in the bellies of illegals or even of their dogs. There is a tale of smugglers anesthetizing rattlesnakes, expertly opening them, inserting necessarily narrow cargos of cocaine, and then rushing them to pet shops over the border.

Along the total border from Brownsville, Texas, to San Diego, the three and a half thousand agents of the border patrol captured about a million illegals from Mexico in the year before I passed along the border. They sent back eight million *nondocumentados*, people who'd simply crossed from Mexico without documents and who returned voluntarily but under strong persuasion by the border police.

So though Douglas *gives* that impression of having slept serenely and affluently, glutted by sun, ever since the day Geronimo gave in and was shunted off for the rest of his life to Fort Marion, Florida, and then to Fort Sill, Oklahoma, the serenity may be fraudulent. The border at Douglas looks cosier and more orderly than it does in Brownsville or Tijuana or southeast of San Diego. But the tunnel stands as evidence of a strange and probably perpetual traffic here on Arizona's quietest border.

TOMBSTONE IS down there in desolate Cochise County, and most travelers do a loop down to it on their way to the New Mexico border east of Douglas. In fact for some, Tombstone is Arizona's premier tourist attraction.

The town stands for the disorders which delayed Arizona's and New Mexico's admission to statehood and which contradictorily foisted upon them venal and mediocre federal officials as a result. In gun-mad America, Tombstone is of course also a shrine. The unfounded credo which brings the buses in is that a good man with a good gun can bring order to a mad town. Tombstone was crowded with members of the National Rifle Association, wearing gun-club caps and plaid trousers and asking politely why I had skis on top of my vehicle. They pointed up by so doing another of the dangers of writing about travel: No one writing about travel travels like a real traveler. You travel equipped and overloaded in ways which have nothing to do with the normal leisures and reasonable itineraries of the travel of normal people.

Tombstone is a byword for the lawlessness of the West and a Station of the Cross for those who believe that selfless lawmen brought civic harmony. By renouncing the practice of plural marriage, Utah managed to achieve statehood before the end of the nineteenth century, whereas monogamous Arizona paid a heavy price for the reputation which Tombstone and similar places gave it.

You will find local historians who will argue that the region was unjustly deprived of statehood. Other regions had been as lawless in their time. Arizona's unjustly acquired reputation, they say, was a matter of the region's period of lawlessness coinciding with a more surefire pistol technology. Since there were fewer misfires, there was a serious death toll.

Similarly, you hear the old argument about federal officials: They had no attachment to the land or the community; they belonged to the highest bidder; they recruited rough trade to argue the interests of high bidders they'd attached themselves to. Federal and other officials themselves therefore fueled the anarchy.

Much of this analysis applies to Tombstone's most notorious event. The shoot-out at the O.K. Corral was

•

between two sets of undesirables representing two sets of corrupt officials, one set being based on Cochise County officialdom and the other on the clique which controlled the city of Tombstone.

The Earp brothers, of whom there were five altogether, and of whom three took part in the shoot-out near the O.K. Corral, along with their consumptive sidekick Doc Holliday, an enthusiastic but utterly unqualified dentist, were all minor officials of and enforcers for the city of Tombstone's Republican mayor and newspaper editor, John P. Clum. The opposing Clantons were associates of the county sheriff, Behan, who was making his pile as county tax collector and who sent all printing work the way of the Democratic *Nugget* rather than to Clum's *Tombstone Epitaph*. Behan had an alliance with, a tolerance for the Clanton family and for their associates, the McLourys, who were all cattle thieves and who sold stolen beef to the booming restaurants and boardinghouses of Tombstone. This at a time when Tombstone was such an extraordinary mining town that it rivaled Phoenix.

In fact the place got its name not at all as a result of the hair-trigger nature of life there. It was named by a mining engineer, Ed Schiefflin, who discovered silver carbonate there in 1878. He had traveled into the region against the advice of associates, since the Apache had just broken out of their grim San Carlos reservation and were looking for someone to punish for their decline. Schiefflin gave the place its name for ironic, not for gunplay reasons. In fact, he was told that "the only stone you will find in those Indian-infested hills will be your tombstone."

Venal Wyatt Earp would later parlay what happened at the O.K. Corral into a national reputation as the quintessential marshal, the unblinking avatar of order. In fact when Wyatt with his two brothers and Doc Holliday encountered the Clantons and McLourys near the O.K. Corral in late October 1881, Wyatt was merely deputy city marshal to his brother Virgil.

Both parties to the shoot-out had earlier thrown accusations of stagecoach robberies at each other, and both camps had a toll of grievances. The Clantons, for example, knew that Wyatt Earp had deliberately seduced their friend Sheriff Behan's mistress.

The shoot-out was over in no time—even the reenactments people line up to see in Tombstone today have to be surrounded with a great deal of palaver and gun tricks, since the event itself was so momentary. As the *Tombstone Epitaph* described it the day after, "Three men hurled into eternity in the duration of a moment." Nor was it, however brief in duration, the quick-draw stuff that brings the tourist buses in. Wheezy Doc Holliday didn't take any chances with one of the McLoury boys who was unarmed and was reaching for the rifle on his saddle. He shot him dead on the spot.

There was a trial of the Earps and an acquittal, and there were reprisals. Virgil was crippled in one ambush. The other Earp brother from the O.K. Corral, Morgan, was shot dead in another. Wyatt himself was shot at from the windows of a billiard parlor. In riposte, the Earps and Holliday shot two men whom they suspected of killing Morgan. But at last they were forced out of town by civic outrage and the force of firepower arrayed against them.

B OOT HILL Cemetery is entered via a gift shop, but
it is certainly an authentic cemetery—the participants
in a late nineteenth century bank holdup, including a
teenage boy, hanged from lamp posts in Tombstone, are
buried here, as are mine disaster victims and folk murdered by Mexicans, Apache, lovers, or lovers' husbands.

But despite that, there does seem to be an attempt
to make history cuter than it was. I wonder about the
grave marker on which is inscribed, black paint on a
white base,

Here lies Les Moore
Took three slugs
From a 44
No Les no more.

Busloads of folk guffaw their way around this cemetery. Probably no cemetery on earth produces such hilar-
ity. The men in the plaid pants and the gun-club caps
don't seem very interested in the other Tombstone: industrial and mining Tombstone and its complicated history
and union turbulence. Tombstone and nearby Bisbee
were scenes of extensive copper, silver, and gold mining.
The Million Dollar Stope runs beneath the town, and
more were killed in an explosion in the Lucky Cuss than
ever perished in face-offs in the streets. The International
Workers of the World, the Wobblies, were active here in
the early twentieth century. From Tombstone in 1917,
twelve hundred striking miners were rounded up by state
troopers and dispatched by box car into exile in New
Mexico.

But of the mining disasters and agitation, of all the
complicated endeavor of mining, there is very little visible

•

in Tombstone. You can visit the Good Enough Mine, but there is no Wobblies' Cafe to go along with the Crystal Palace Saloon, with Boot Hill, with the Bird Cage Theater.

Whereas Bisbee, halfway between Tombstone and Douglas, and despite its ungraphic name, is a far more genuinely delightful little town. Though it no doubt had its share of violent face-offs, its atmosphere is utterly different.

When the mining stopped in the 1960s and all the miners moved out at once, putting their houses up for sale, artists and writers moved in. They are lucky to live in that high, dry climate, in a town of un–Disneyfied charm.

I have seen Tombstone, and once was enough. But charming Bisbee is one of those wonderfully odd old American towns. It keeps to a hillside, and the old hotels and boardinghouses of the mining years are everywhere. The Copper Queen, named for a famous lode, is a superb-looking hotel, as fine as any example of Coloradan mining-boom architecture. Horace Tabor at his apogee would have willingly booked a room there. Bisbee has not been able to mulch its past. The past is still unexpunged and unexorcised there, in Bisbee's steep and narrow streets which contain real shops and nary a boutique or a T-shirt factory. The towns I like are the ones where the local museum is like the one in that other great, steep-streeted copper town, Jerome, far to the north on Mingus Mountain; a museum run by serious-minded volunteers from the historical society; a museum where the inventory of purchasable souvenirs is staid and small.

Bisbee probably attracts some drug dealers too, because of its proximity to the border. Sad to recount, it

•

would be a more atmospheric place to live on foul-gotten gains than Douglas.

Also, the great abandoned copper mine of the area endears one with its gentle, nonmacho name. It is called the Lavender Pit.

IF YOU see Bisbee on your last afternoon in Arizona, as I did, before skirting down to aforementioned Douglas and Agua Prieta; and head up through barren hills, which nonetheless pleasingly shift color throughout the day, to New Mexico by way of Rodeo, you go with that same wistful sense that you have acquired up in the northeast, with the Navajo and the Hopi and other Arizonans, and in the places haunted by the Anasazi relatives, the Hohokam. Arizona is a complicated equation. Arizona is worthy of an intenser and intenser study. Arizona is plump with what you might call gothic ironies, and of vistas which not only exhilarate you but—if you'll forgive the portentousness—put the big question: your relativity to these immense features, and the relativity, the accident, of your own culture.

Creeping toward New Mexico, with all its promised ironies and splendors, I felt a sort of anxiety. I assured myself that nostalgia was unnecessary. Arizona and New Mexico were the same country, were once the one province called New Spain.

But the question is: Will the experience of the region which is here drawing to a close on the lonely roads through Chiricahua and Apache ever be repeated? This is the travel-book blues.

•

NINE

The Province of the Sun

NE NIGHT the last of the at-large Apache were being conducted by rail at the hands of a grateful federal authority through New Mexico and toward detention at Fort Marion, Florida. At Deming, on the Mimbres River, which gave its name (Mimbresino) to a form of prehistoric pottery, some cowboys rushed the train and tried to lynch chiefs Nana and Geronimo.

As in northwestern Colorado, in New Mexico we are in a region where the frontier and the present are telescoped. Many New Mexicans who were children on the night Geronimo's train was mobbed were only young men and women at the time of Pancho Villa's last incursion into the United States, across the Deming Plain in 1916. The same people were only in their late middle or early old age by the stage that—some way to the north of Deming—the Manhattan Project moved into the finger mesas of Los Alamos to brew up those little portions of Arma-

•

geddon whimsically named Little Boy and Fat Man.

That is the nature of New Mexico, palpable every-where. The frontier and the future at one gulp. If you know the right people in Abiquiu—not far from Los Alamos and the town where Georgia O'Keeffe settled—you can see at Easter the Penitentes fixed to their crosses in the pasturages and bean fields. New Mexico members of that secret devotional society also allow themselves to be flogged with cactus whips, the spines needing to be pulled from the flesh to prevent suppuration and to pro-long the ascetic passion. And at Socorro, the Very Large Array radio telescopes, set on rails miles long and aimed into the heavens, vastly scan light from the remotest time: the very roots, that is, of light and time.

The slackest and least endowed of all Spanish and Mexican provinces, New Mexico then brought us the newest and most absolute era, the era in which funda-mental folly could threaten not simply some local disaster but an end to the planet. In the gazetteer of all our minds, therefore, New Mexico glows with a certain radioactive threat.

God knows what they—the military, the scientists—are all doing in the deserts near Alamagordo or in the mesas of Los Alamos now, but you can be sure that it is as mysterious and many times more dangerous than intentions Geronimo ever harbored.

BEFORE I begin, there is a housekeeping—or rather a bookkeeping—matter to be attended to. The Spaniards called all the characteristic settlements occupied by sed-entary Indians *pueblos*—villages. The uppercase Pueblo

Indians could strictly speaking include all these: the Hopi of Arizona, the Zuni of northwestern New Mexico, and all the Tewa and Keresan-speaking people in northern and central New Mexico, especially those spread in pueblos along the Rio Grande. Of these Rio Grande pueblos, Taos pueblo—beloved of Mabel Dodge Luhan and Georgia O'Keeffe and visited and ambiguously admired by D. H. and Frieda Lawrence—is arguably the most famous. In practice, the pueblo-dwelling Hopi are called the Hopi, the pueblo-dwelling Zuni are called the Zuni, and only the pueblo-dwelling Rio Grande people are called the Pueblo. Perhaps I explain all this so you will know—as with the Anasazi–Sinagua–Hohokam phenomenon—it is permissible to be confused.

IT IS little wonder that New Mexico's history is so readable. It is like the histories of convict settlements in Australia—one is left in a state of bewilderment at the way people hung on; at the way the country and its native peoples could at any time have canceled European administration and even managed to do so for more than a decade.

The Spanish connection in New Mexico began with an organization which would continue through New Mexico's history—the Order of Friars Minor, the Franciscans. The classic adobe mission churches found in the pueblos and the oldest mission church of all, San Miguel on the east side of Santa Fe, owe their architecture to missionaries of this order, who in turn owe it back to the Pueblo themselves.

A certain friar named Fray Marcos seems to have

been a more erratic member of the Franciscan order. He had been to Peru with Pizarro. He entered New Spain, present Arizona and New Mexico, in 1539, and sighted the Zuni pueblos from the west. He should have perhaps visited them and verified what he was about to tell the European world about them. But one of his party, a Moor, had been slaughtered in Hawikuh, a now-abandoned pueblo on the Zuni reservation, only a few miles from the present Arizona–New Mexico border. So Fray Marcos's resolve to look more closely was undermined.

He returned to Mexico with unsubstantiated news of seven golden cities, the Seven Cities of Cíbola. His Peruvian experience had raised his expectations of the value of Indian kingdoms!

Francisco Coronado, the governor of Nueva Galicia, as Sonora seems to have been then called, was inflamed by Fray Marcos's lively tale. He took off for New Spain the following year. He had a large company of men and Marcos for a guide. His journey would be an estimable one. Yet the account has the surreal quality of the hunt for the grail as portrayed by Monty Python.

The party's arrival at Hawikuh, first of Fray Marcos's seven cities, disabused Coronado. Detachments under his lieutenants were sent off in a number of directions following Indian rumors. One party under the young Don Lopez de Cardenas found Tusayan, a pueblo near the Grand Canyon. Its remains still stand near the eastern end of the present national park. Cardenas's group was led by Hopi to the rim of the Grand Canyon. They cursed it for being too deep to fetch water from. It doesn't seem to have astounded them with its scope. Their souls were set on other possibilities.

•

Meanwhile the Zuni of Hawikuh had shown toward Coronado and Marcos and the others a common trait of indigenous people: as a matter of politeness to tell the stranger anything he wants to hear. A Pueblo Indian the Spaniards nicknamed Bigotes—"Whiskers"—arrived in Hawikuh and told Coronado about the great cities of Piguex to the east, along the region's great river. Bigotes's promises weren't as fulsome as Fray Marcos's had been, but Coronado had everything to gain by checking them out. The absence of riches in Cíbola fed ever more strongly the Spanish expectation that the riches had to be some damn place.

Led by Bigotes, Coronado came east to the great mesa-top pueblo of Acoma, which is still there on its red mesa. Then he moved on to what is now the Rio Grande. He named it the Rio del Norte. Along it he found strung twelve Tiwa- and Tewa-speaking pueblos and others still down toward what would become the site of Albuquerque.

Coronado and his men moved into one of the pueblos, clearing it of Indians and living off grain requisitioned from them. He had no ethnographic enthusiasm for the place. He spent a disappointed and miserable winter. Bigotes had joined Fray Marcos in isolation, but a Plains indian nicknamed the Turk, a man who had been living with the Pueblo Indians at Pecos, told Coronado what he was still willing to hear. There *was* an emperor and an empire to the east. There were trees from which golden bells hung. There were gold-prowed galleons on orderly canals, and the commonest utensil was also of gold.

It is again wonderful that these hardheaded and venal men could be so carried away by the persiflage of a plausible Indian; that having believed and then discredited Fray Marcos, they could then be snowed by Bigotes and then by the Turk.

IN AUSTRALIAN exploration, for the first eighty years of European occupation, there was a European delusion similar to that which beset the Spanish in New Mexico. In the Australian case, the expectation was of an interior sea. The apparent aridity of the continent couldn't last—so the European mind said anyhow—all the way through. It is interesting that in the case of New Mexico/New Spain, there was an expectation too that a Strait of Anian would be found out there to the west of Santa Fe, a mythical west coast this side of California, with unimagined ports along it.

This on top of what could be called the Montezuma Syndrome, the Inca Supposition. It was expected of new desolations that they yield golden kings, just as it was expected that they should yield an inner sea. Coronado did not easily shake off either idea.

The tendency toward fantastic hope is implicit in the air of New Mexico even now. The ambience is a faith-promoting one, as the crosses of Abiquiu would suggest. The enormous aridity of its south and center, the inhuman scale of its north–south mountains, the Sacreamento, the exquisite Sangre de Cristos, the San Juan. It is impossible to believe that nullities lie on their far sides. This is an immensity which cries out to be plushly filled. If you were going to believe that, somewhere even closer to the core of the continent than the Rio Grande already is, golden bells are hanging from trees and golden bows

•

are cutting water, then northern New Mexico is surely the place to believe it.

Marc Simmons, a New Mexico historian, complains that American history books are very dismissive about the Spaniards—they portray them as venal. Whereas no one human could come upon the Rio Grande—after all that desert—and see those civilized pueblos and those great mountains and not expect the best, not expect to encounter a Khan.

AND SO the Turk led three hundred robust Spaniards right across New Mexico, out of the land of the pueblos, across the sloping plateau called the Llano Estacado, the high Staked Plains, and then on into the prairies, looking for the empire the Turk called Quivira. Discovering a settlement of Wichita Indians in what is now Kansas, and confronted by a chieftain whose only splendor was a copper plate worn round the neck, Coronado despaired and celebrated his bitterness by executing the Turk. It seems to have been a savage recompense for mere boosting. For Babbitry and boosting are venial and universal crimes in the Southwest, where even towns which have nothing else to say for themselves boast of their average days of unabashed sunlight or their occasional historic or geographic accident.

For what can Columbus in Luna County, New Mexico, say for itself except that Pancho Villa once killed seventeen Americans there? What can Artesia in Eddy County say except that it is the turnoff to beautiful Carlsbad?

After the Coronado and other intrusions, an imperial

edict of 1573 forbade unauthorized expeditions into New Spain, but New Mexico's capacity to attract exorbitant and doomed figures continued. Where better to sit than in the lounge of the old hostelry, La Fonda, in Santa Fe, or at the table of a coffee shop on the plaza and read in Marc Simmons' history of the gold-crazed Juan de Oñate. Oñate was a middle-aged and middle-ranking military official when appointed governor of New Mexico in 1598, with authorization to explore all its coasts and ports. Permanent European presence was to begin with him.

I believe that if he had been Anglo-Saxon his tale would be a fable, a moral tale in majority America. He was the son of a Basque mining tycoon from Zacatecas in central Mexico and of a woman related both to Cortez and Montezuma. He was therefore what the Spaniards called a *criollo* (Creole), a non-*gachupino* (Spanish-born), and tainted with Indian blood. Yet the mythology of golden kingdoms was, in plainest terms, in his blood. He hit the Rio Grande just south of El Paso del Norte, the pass to the north, but mountains forced him away from the river into an awful stretch of alkali desert which—with greater aptness than he ever suspected—he named Jornada del Muerto, the journey of the dead.

This is a terrible, white-gray wilderness amongst mountains, desert despite its terrible thunderstorms, and grimly sad in winter, as if it has been in training since the Pleistocene for its role as the place where the world would begin to end. Three hundred and forty-seven years after Oñate's thirsty passage of this stretch, the first test firing of an atomic bomb would occur there, at the site which even the secularized scientists named Trinity.

Getting a genial response from the Pueblo at what Oñate and his friars named Santo Domingo—it is still a

pueblo on the west bank of the Rio Grande—they kept
north and made a settlement in a village near the point
where the Chama enters the Rio Grande and called the
place San Gabriel. This was to the north of present Santa
Fe, near San Juan pueblo, about halfway between Santa
Fe, that is, and Taos.

Though Oñate went right over to Zuni looking for
minerals, he found none. A large party of his men, including his aristocratic and pure-Spanish nephew, were lured
up to startling Acoma pueblo, set on its enormous rose
red platform of rock, and were slaughtered. Some of the
hidalgos jumped from the precipice rather than face the
final strokes of the Acoma people.

The great slaughter of Acoma that followed at
Oñate's order is remembered to this day. Oñate killed
somewhere near eight hundred Acoma people. All males
over the age of twenty-five had a foot cut off. Two Hopi
who had been visiting Acoma at the time of the opening
attack on the Spaniards lost a hand apiece. Sixty Acoma
girls were exiled to convents in Mexico City.

This pattern of exacting punishments would be repeated elsewhere. Every surviving pueblo has memories
of historic massacre and retribution.

You hear chance references from people you talk to
in the many pueblos along the Rio Grande, and east and
west of it too, about the people of other pueblos. It does
seem that in the collective mind of a given pueblo, each
of the other pueblos are marked by a specific characteristic: There are the most stubborn, the most spendthrift,
the most riotous, the most genial, the most theologically
unyielding, the most given to song, the biggest liars. The
references are fascinatingly oblique, because a certain loy-
alty runs between the Pueblo Indians. Many of the pueb-

•

los are related by blood, tongue, and by shared ritual. That community of spirit would be demonstrated under the Spanish. The only people they will let themselves be frankly contemptuous of are Apache and Navajo.

In this catalog of special pueblo characteristics, it seems that the Acoma people have always been amongst the most resistant. There would come a time—and it is narrated in Willa Cather's *Death Comes for the Archbishop*—when they would even throw the missionaries off the red cliffs of the pueblo. Acoma still looks unbreachable, as you drive west over the gray plains and look up to its dominant red sandstone.

The viceroy Oñate seems to have become unhinged in the end. Complaints were made to Mexico about his assault on the wives of other members of his party. Intelligence reached his superiors concerning his murders not so much of Indians as of dissenters amongst the colonists. He was recalled. Spain would have wound up the enterprise except that the Franciscans were making good progress at Isleta and Santo Domingo.

As he traveled home over the Jornado del Muerto to face trial, his party was attacked by Apache and his beloved twenty-two-year-old son, the boy who was to have inherited all the titles Oñate had once believed would accrue to him as a reward for his New Mexican adventure, was killed.

Like the atomic scientists three hundred and forty or so years later, Oñate went to New Mexico with fixed objectives and crept away with results too terrible to be frankly looked upon.

THE PLACE WHERE SOULS ARE BORN

OÑATE'S SUCCESSOR, Peralta, made Santa Fe the Southwest's fanciest city. He began building the New villa to the south of San Gabriel and on a side river of the Rio Grande. He may have named the planned town after Santa Fe in Spain, a grid layout town created by Ferdinand and Isabella. Or it may have been a statement of intent: to stay until the Holy Faith had penetrated all the pueblos, even the ones we still see set on sky-high rocks in desert places.

The Palace of the Governors was built in the main square and has been there, in its various incarnations, ever since. It is the oldest European building in all this immensity of American space. If I had to think of an image of the Southwest, other of course than the cliff dwellings of Mesa Verde, this venerable adobe sprawl would qualify.

There is little sense though, as you come up to Santa Fe from the south, that you are approaching an early center of European civilization in North America. Santa Fe is besieged by a light industrial perimeter as squalid as any in America. Motels and fast-food franchises and malls and tire barns crowd along roads named promisingly: Cerrillos, Agua Fria, Don Diego Avenue, Galisteo Street, and Don Gaspar Avenue. Even the old Santa Fe Trail which comes in from the south might as well be some ugly strip in Los Angeles.

It is as you near the narrow channel of the Santa Fe River that the town turns into the expected Santa Fe; the picturesque middle where—sadly—very few Santa Feans can afford to live.

This is the bijou part of town, which all the perimeter schlock serves and to which Americans and others come for its antiquity and its style. Is there another city of this size on the American mainland which has such artistic and decorative cachet? At this center, the visitors are in contact with the roots of European experience in North America, and from this center, they can travel out to the pueblos, to the roots of human experience.

SANTA FE shrugged off easily the first Yankee contact. This first mere touch was made by young Lieutenant Zebulon Pike, who built a stockade on a tributary of the Rio Grande in 1806, believing it was a tributary of the Red River, and who was taken as a Spanish captive to Santa Fe and genially treated. Pike's renown of course lives not down here in New Mexico but further north, in the gold-bearing mountains of the Front Range of the Rockies, where Pike's Peak overwhelms the eye when the clouds don't hold it fast.

The Spanish families who were there when Pike visited are the folk who these days—like the old Hispanic families of Tucson—despise the come-lately immigrants. There are families in Albuquerque and Santa Fe and Taos who date their origins back to Oñate's settlement. In with Oñate, out with Otermín in 1680, back with Vargas, and living there by the river, in the desert and mountains ever since. No wonder they feel a little *amour propre*!

But American wranglers, arriving here from Missouri, at the end of the Santa Fe trail when Santa Fe still belonged to Mexico, were as contemptuous of the Palace of the Governors and the inns as Pike was. They were all just adobe, they would say. The Santa Fe trail diarist Josiah Gregg complains of "the dust and manure-filled plaza" in a passage which is on display in the palace. The palace was just adobe, it was long and low.

How extraordinary that the material of necessity—adobe—has now become the material of style. Now that everyone has a passion for Santa Fee style, nobody feels like Gregg. People look at the palace and note how apposite it is to the brown-red hills around. The suburbs to the fashionable north of the town, whatever they're built of, feel bound to mimic the adobe style of the palace, as does the beautiful Museum of Fine Arts next door.

Now Pike's great great grandchildren go stamping across the plaza with their copies of Mabel Dodge Luhan and Tony Hillerman and Willa Cather in hand, believing doggedly they have come for the deepest experience America can offer.

CATHER'S BOOK, *Death Comes for the Archbishop*, is a big seller here. It is based on the history of the French Archbishop Lamy, who lived in New Mexico while the Apache still dominated the country and the imagination.

Lamy disapproved of the plaza which modern Americans enthuse about. He only wanted, writes Cather, "a tawny adobe town with a few green trees . . . but the year 1880 had begun a period of incongruous American building. Now, half the plaza square was still adobe, and half was flimsy wooden buildings with double porches, scroll work and jackstraw posts and bannisters painted white. Father Latour said the wooden houses which had so distressed him in Ohio, had followed him. All this was

•

quite wrong for the Cathedral he had been so many years
in building . . ."

I have to disagree with the archbishop, supreme New
Mexican patriot chauvinist though he be. It seems right
that the two cultures abut like this in Santa Fe, the great
American terminus of the Southwest. It seems right that
America laps its way up the Santa Fe trail to the east
side of the square and meets the adobe, all the way from
Chihuahua, in solid commercial comity.

Navajo blankets and Zuni jewelry and Pueblo pottery
offer themselves from the windows of those Yankee
buildings Archbishop Latour, a.k.a. Lamy, despised. Then,
on the western side, along the veranda of the Palace,
which is called the Portal in New Mexican argot, perhaps
a hundred registered Indian vendors sit on blankets every
morning. Many of them are women. They are largely from
the pueblos north and south of Santa Fe—Nambe, Picuris
(which was discovered by the Spanish in its hidden valley
very late—1751—and which has never signed any treaties
and remains self-ruling), San Ildefonso, Santa Clara,
Jemez, Tesuque, and Taos. San Ildefonso, an impeccably
kept pueblo to the north, was the home of the great pot-
ter, Maria Martínez, whose pots are for sale, if at all, only
in the galleries off the plaza. Also represented under the
Portal are Cochiti and Santa Domingo pueblos, which lie
to the south of Santa Fe and which provide much of the
silver jewelry sold.

There are even a few Navajo and Hopi dealers.

But the portal is not as informal an arrangement as
it looks. All the vendors of the portal are licensed by the
Portal Committee. A Palace of the Governors guide to
buying under the Portal advises purchasers, "Remember
that authentic Indian art and crafts are labor inten-

sive. . . . Under the Portal, where the vendors are subject to specific guidelines encouraging traditional techniques, the quality is regulated." What are called "Portal Program Regulations" require that every piece sold carry the maker's mark. The average quality of the jewelry here seems excellent.

To walk under the Portal it is of course possible to evoke a little of how journeyers felt after they had survived the Comanche and the Apache and the alkaline water holes of the Santa Fe trail or of the long journey north from Sonora and come at last to this place.

YOU LOOK at the Pueblo under the Portal, these extraordinary Anasazi-descended people whose souls the Spanish Franciscans harried, whose validity D. H. Lawrence questioned, and such is their repute that you are amazed to find that ordinary portable radios sit with them on their rugs. These people have had relative success in the face of the European onset; as distinct from the relative failure of the nomadic Indians, particularly those who gave the Europeans the most sustained trouble, the Apache and the Comanche. The people of the pueblos are—like the Hopi—the great lasters. As well, they gave the Spaniards their greatest shock.

The impulse of our age is generally to approve of tribespeople, as long as you don't live too close to them. D. H. Lawrence was imbued with the impulses of *his* age and pretty much benignly discounted the Taos Pueblo people. He thought it was a bit indulgent of Mabel Dodge Luhan, the New Mexico writer, to marry one of them, a certain Tony Luhan. Lawrence was largely tolerant, of course, but dismissive of Pueblo efforts to achieve divine grace through ritual.

Yet in order to survive, Pueblo culture had to outlast a number of malign conditions and events. It has had to survive, for example, the *encomienda*, a tax of grain and blankets, imposed by the Spanish. It survived and resented the *repartimiento*: forced labor for Spanish landlords. The Pueblo suffered the suppression of their religion under Governor Trevino, and the people of the Tewa-speaking villages north of Santa Fe saw their ritual leaders—*caciques*, the Spaniards called them, a word they had brought with them from Cuba—imprisoned, some of them hanged, and others flogged.

Pueblo culture had to survive the results of the Pueblo uprising, the reoccupation, the arrival of the Yankee army, and federal attempts to undermine traditional ownership by law.

The tale of the uprising is extrordinary and is still intimately commemorated along the Rio Grande. The leaders were genuine ideologues and had been flogged in the plaza the year before the rebellion for encouraging the old religion. In 1680 a San Juan pueblo *cacique* named Popé, a Picuris pueblo leader named Luis Tapatu, and a Santo Domingo Indian named Catiti instigated a popular revolt. The Pueblo drove the Spaniards out of New Mexico altogether, occupying the palace for twelve years and building their own ceremonial kiva there. In sitting under the portal, the Pueblo artists are merely in the shade of walls within which their ancestors exercised a considerable, twelve-year governorship.

This Popé was a Pueblo absolutist. He sent Indians into the Santa Fe river to wash the traces of baptism from themselves with soap weed. He ordered men to put aside the wives they had taken in Christian marriage and marry others. He destroyed clothing, tools, weapons, livestock, carts, and fruit trees. He was the leader of a cultural revolution.

His extreme stance ultimately failed. Generally, the Pueblo resistance to western culture has been—ever since—less clamant than Popé's and far more subtle.

A FRESH viceroy, Vargas, had to take Santa Fe by storm in 1693 and was able to do it because Popé had died and the Pueblo were fragmented.

So a new Spanish occupation began, and in this they've-learned-their-lesson phase, one would have thought that Pueblo life would be easy to extinguish. It very nearly was. Drought, diseases introduced by the Spaniards, and the depredations of the Apache meant that the Pueblo shrunk to a minute population of about fourteen thousand people by 1700. They were therefore ripe for a redemptive overturning of their Indian minds followed by a merciful extinction. Such are the odds the Pueblo jewelers in the portal have beaten.

The common threat from the Apache was accentuated within ten years of the recovery of Santa Fe by the Spaniards through the arrival of another raiding tribe, the Comanche. Both tribes and their raids are part of the received memory of New Mexicans and West Texans even now. You meet people who still consider these non-Pueblo Indians the Antichrist. A New Mexican said to me that he believed Apache society was of its essence sadistic. I asked whether it only seemed that way because the Apache were at war for their survival. I argued that there

•

may have been Vietnamese villagers who considered, on the evidence before them, that American society was essentially sadistic, but they would have been wrong. Perhaps we were misjudging the Apache on similarly limited evidence.

My reason for arguing that way was an Apache poem, written during the tribal decline and mourning a dead child, which seemed to combine the finest human sentiments.

> She was small and warm
> her hands like cotton
> her face like ropes
> her hair like a waterfall
> her face like a stone
> her mind like the sky
> her life like a river
> her death like a fever of sorrow
> her memory small and warm

Under attack from the Apache, the Spaniards and the Pueblo were driven closer together. Every family suffered attrition. The one break in the continuous tension was the yearly Taos trade fair, when in autumn Comanche, Ute, Apache, Navajo, Pueblo, Spaniards, Frenchmen, and Yankees, all met to do business in a pasture near the pueblo in an atmosphere devoted to temporary fraternity.

The Taos trade fair was a remarkable institution, a festival and a truce, an indemnity against slaughter and prosecution. The raiding tribes actually brought in their hostages to be ransomed, all without penalty of law. This practice of festival and sanctuary in one event continued long after the Yankees took over.

Outside that though, the threat from the nomads was

so intense about the time the War of Independence was being pursued in the east of the continent, the Spaniards voluntarily locked themselves in Taos pueblo with the Indians, feeling secure only in the Taos people's concentrated township.

At last Governor Anza made a lasting peace with the Comanche, so enduring in its effects that even in the days of Kit Carson, Mexicans were safe from Comanche when Yankees weren't.

Today there are few places on earth where tribalism still prevails so successfully, in the midst of what we are pleased to call the developed world, as it does in Pueblo New Mexico. Compared to other tribes and despite evidence of the inroads of booze and cultural dislocation of all shades, the Pueblo and the Zuni are not merely a sad remnant, panhandling for a shot of whiskey. They no doubt have historic and current grievances, but they also have their special public stature as survivors and as artists. For indigenes, it is not always so elsewhere on earth: It does not appear to be that way for Aboriginals in Alice Springs, say, at Australia's heart, and certainly not for the Ute in Cortez, Colorado.

Throughout, the Pueblo sustained their clan systems, their annual ceremonies, and what you might call their kachina-driven view of the year; of all of which the Spaniards, the Mexicans, and the Yankees have in relay been disapproving for centuries.

IN THE plaza where New Mexico's great shift occured, I sat on a park bench in the dry air and read, utterly captivated, of the processes by which New Mexico be-

•

came North American. After Mexican independence, more and more Yankee traders moved into Santa Fe and the Spanish *villa* of Taos, and so did Yankee trappers. The local Mexicans came to believe they owed more to the oncoming Yankees than they did to distant Mexico City. Officials such as the governor of Chihuahua tried to stiffen their Hispanic resistance. "Do you know who the Texans are? They are adventurers who despise you as barbarians, weak minded and corrupt men. They blaspheme your religion and scoff at your pious customs; they are grasping merchants who envy the fertility of your lands, the richness of your minds, and the clemency of your weather . . ."

But in Santa Fe, Mexicans made their own arrangements without listening to the bombast from Chihuahua or Mexico City.

In 1837 Pueblo and Mexicans north of Santa Fe felt they had so little in common with the Mexico City-appointed viceroy that they rose and decapitated the man. These same people welcomed Kit Carson, Santa Fe trail refugee, when he married the Taos girl Josepha Jaramillo and settled in Taos in the house which is still a museum to his memory.

President James K. Polk, fired by manifest destiny and looking for a *casus belli*, found it when in the spring of 1846 Mexican troops from Chihuahua crossed the Rio Grande and attacked an American force in Texas. Colonel Stephen Watts Kearny was given the task of marching into the Southwest and taking Santa Fe. His force was made up of three hundred army regulars and twelve hundred Missouri volunteers. Gusted along by newspaper talk, they marched with a great certainty.

•

Oh what a joy to fight the dons,
And wallop fat Armijo!
So clear the way to Santa Fe!
With that we all agree, Oh!

Governor Armijo decided not to put up the resistance he had planned for Apache Canyon to the east of Santa Fe and fled instead to El Paso, leaving the acting governor, Alarid, to surrender New Mexico to Kearny.

It is recorded in the Palace of the Governors that Kearny went to a lot of trouble to make the locals feel comfortable with Yankee rule, even attending Mass and carrying a candle in a religious procession. His deputy, Colonel Doniphan, stayed on after Kearny had gone to California, and received Sterling Price with the Mormon Battalion as reinforcements.

The Americans would feel uneasy for some time about acquiring the Mexican population who went along with these new Southwest territories. It frightened their solid Wasp sensibilities, and perhaps they saw in it the unanswered questions which still grow from the geographic continuity between the American Southwest and Mexico.

WHILE DONIPHAN marched on as far as the city of Chihuahua, General Sterling Price had to face a rebellion in Taos against the American Governor Charles Bent. The Indians at Taos pueblo were involved in the rising.

In Bent Street north of the plaza of Taos, the slaughtered governor's house remains now as a museum. All the ordinariness of its furnishings—its rockers and sofas and sideboards, its lamps and hung whips and displayed Colt revolvers, casts a homeliness over Charles Bent. But his death was not quite homely. Mexicans and a number of Pueblo had been planning an insurrection for Santa Fe and Taos since Kearny arrived toward the end of the previous summer. They had resented Mexico City's distant authority, but now they resented Yankee arrogance.

In Taos the rebels are believed to have been inflamed by an extraordinary priest, Antonio Martínez. Martínez is a villain in Willa Cather's *Death Comes for the Archbishop*, bringing great anguish to that good, solid, Gallican young man from France, Bishop Latour. In real life, Martínez's enemy was Bishop Lamy, on whom Latour is based. It is interesting that Cather feels bound to give Lamy a fictional name in the novel, whereas Martínez comes to us under his real one.

There is a painting of him in the Palace of the Governors, and he looks princely and worldly. Martínez was an ambiguous man—venal and generous, charging heavily for the sacraments but profligate with his charities. He would ultimately be excommunicated by Archbishop Lamy, and even in that he saw himself as defender of the Mexican way. He would be elected to represent the leading Anglo and Hispanic citizens of New Mexico in an appeal to congress demanding an end to the military government. But his own demagoguery had brought it down on New Mexico in the first place.

Bent's house was invaded by dark. The crowded terror of that night is palpable in the narrow, low-ceilinged hallway. In this tight space just around the corner from Kit Carson's house, bullets and arrows were poured into

•

Bent's body and his scalp hacked away. The sheriff of Taos and business partners in a large land grant Bent had managed to acquire also perished appallingly in the house. The rebels then marched on eastward to Las Vegas—the New Mexico version of it, not the scabrous Nevada one—and were routed there. The remnants came tumbling back to the fortified pueblo of Taos.

You can still see, quite legible on the edge of Taos pueblo, the effects of the siege which developed then. The Franciscans had had to build their churches as potential fortresses, and the Pueblo and Mexican rebels prepared to stand in the church of San Geronimo, which stood on the western side of the great pueblo. Amongst the troops Sterling Price led to attack the rebels were sixty-five enflamed Yankee trappers gathered by Bent's trader friend, Céran St. Vrain.

The Yankee assault on Taos pueblo and on the church of San Geronimo degenerated into a massacre nearly worthy of New Mexico's first viceroy, Oñate. Indians and Mexicans who perished there are buried in the ruins of San Geronimo, along with the pueblo's more recent dead. Fifteen surviving rebels were hanged; an enormous number for a small community.

Such savage confrontations perhaps provoked that great epigrammatist General William Tecumseh Sherman, razer of the South turned Indian fighter, to utter another famed dictum: that the United States should declare war on the Mexicans and make them take New Mexico back.

But once more, all this questioning and turbulence the Pueblo have witnessed and survived. They have witnessed and survived more than one hundred European governors in the so-called palace! They have witnessed the transplanting of the Navajo from Arizona to Bosque

Redondo by General Kit Carson of Taos. They have witnessed the occupation of Santa Fe by the Confederates
in 1862; the rebels were shocked to find the walls of the
Palace of the Governors decorated with the ears of
Apache and scalps draped on Federal Governor Connel-
ly's desk, but they dished out some dirt of their own and,
being mainly Texans, weren't too impressed by Indians
of any stripe.

And the Pueblo survived the Apache too. After 1874
the Apache were meant to be confined to San Carlos in
Arizona, but they continued to break out under Victorio,
Nana, and Geronimo and did not finally surrender—in
the foothills of the beautiful Sacramentos, east of Alamo-
gordo—until 1886. A memorial cairn on the edge of the
Mescalero Apache reservation marks the place.

The Pueblo always had this advantage over the nomadic tribes: They lived still in the places they had always
lived. Their connection with *their* earth, the connection
which in the case of the Apache and Comanche was broken in the late nineteenth century, remained intact.

In the early twentieth century, the threat they had to
face was the proposed Bursum Act, a federal draft law
which sought to untangle questions of land ownership in
a way which gave preference to European settlers and
which gave state courts total jurisdiction over Pueblo
water rights and land. Mabel Dodge Luhan wrote letters
to D. H. Lawrence about the Bursum Bill and lectured
him about it during his visits to New Mexico until he was
driven to complain about it in a letter to E. M. Forster.
John Collier, the American writer, took up the cause at
her urging. "The old men of the tribe moaned," wrote
Collier of the reading of the Bursum Act, "knowing it
was a sentence of death."

•

The Pueblo now had new and fashionable allies though, the artists and writers of Taos and Santa Fe and then the General Federation of Women's Clubs. The Bursum Bill was withdrawn from Congress, and in 1924 the Pueblo Lands Act was passed, recognizing the Pueblo Indian land rights which had prevailed under the Spanish administration. F.D.R. would actually appoint John Collier as Commissioner of Indian Affairs.

Campaigns undertaken by the Pueblo and their white admirers would lead by 1970 to the ceding of the sacred Blue Lake watershed on the west of the Sangre de Cristos to the Taos Indians. The major Pueblo ceremonial sites have been secured to them. The nomadic tribes—perhaps with the exception of the Navajo—could rarely claim the same.

TEN

Kachina Music

ITH OUR maps of the Taos pueblo walking tour, we were following the dotted blue line round the back of the north pueblo, along streets which were a quagmire from the early spring thaw. An elderly Taos woman emerged on the roof of the second-story apartment, which also, in the manner of Pueblo pueblos, served as patio of the third-story apartment. She wanted to know what we were doing there? We pleaded the map and its clear blue line.

But she yelled, "You people poke your nose in too much!" We left contritely, even though the map indicated we were supposedly on the right path. Naturally she thought we had maliciously taken the wrong line. I wondered too if she belonged to a faction which opposed the entry of outsiders at all.

There are pueblo factions opposed to tourists. In Santo Domingo, in the season I was there, someone had removed all directions and signs to the pueblo. I was reminded of the fading sign outside Old Oraibi on the Hopi mesas in Arizona:

WARNING

No outside white visitors allowed
Because of your failure to obey the Laws of our Tribe
As well as the Laws of Your Own
This village is hereby closed.

No one could have said that the elderly pueblo woman was in any doubt that this was her place, where her ancestors were buried, and no one could have said what was maliciously said of the Australian aborigines: that in the face of Europeans, she didn't have a pronounced and proper sense of title.

NEW MEXICO'S first literary figure was the Civil War general Lew Wallace, who wrote much of *Ben Hur* in the Governor's Palace. He was in Santa Fe in harsh times and came close on the heels of the Apache-ear collectors. He found the city's long, clear days and dry, cold nights utterly suitable for a literary experiment.

Lew was rather discounted by the D. H. Lawrences and the Mabel Dodge Luhans. He was a manufacturer of popular, pietist fiction. But what a curious combination it was; the book and the place. Rome on the Rio Grande!

New Mexico would develop something like the sort of literary and artistic reputation which early twentieth century Dublin did. This reputation did not attach itself perhaps to Deming or Lordsburg or Las Cruces, which are crass mining towns, nor perhaps to Alamagordo and the regions of test firings, nor to Tucumcari over on old Highway 66. It belonged to northern New Mexico, particularly Santa Fe and Taos. There were extraordinary concatanations of talent in this sweet, mountain-girt amphitheater, and as elsewhere in the state, the fissionable orbs were not always successfully kept separate from each other.

The first European artists had come in 1898—Bert Phillips and Ernest L. Blumenschein. According to the legend, they were both on their way to Mexico from Colorado on a sketching trip when their wagon broke down north of Taos. A walk into Taos to find someone to repair the wheel produced a wonderment which caused Blumenschein and Phillips to settle there.

They would later be joined by Joseph Henry Sharp, Phillips's former teacher. Two is an enthusiasm. Three is a school.

The arrival of the heiress Mabel Dodge Sterne from New York in 1916 inaugurated Taos's and Santa Fe's reputation as a great salon in the foothills of the Rockies. When she began in Taos, she was still married to her third husband, Maurice Sterne, a painter. Later she would marry a Pueblo named Tony Luhan from the Taos pueblo.

In 1922 D. H. Lawrence, writing and tending his incipient tuberculosis in Taormina, Sicily, received from Mabel an extraordinary postal item—a letter about six feet long, rolled up scrollwise, and containing some Indian charms, some perfumed leaves, an Indian medicine named Osha, and a magic necklace from Taos pueblo. She had spotted his talent and wanted him to come to New Mexico.

•

Lawrence first approached New Mexico by way of Australia, a continent which had a similar effect on him as New Mexico would. "If I stayed here six months I should have to stay forever—there's something so remote and far off and utterly indifferent to our European world, in the very air."

It was from New South Wales that he came to New Mexico.

IN TAOS Frieda Lawrence never got on with Mabel, who described Frieda as having "a mouth rather like a gunman." But Mabel had definite concepts of what she needed from Lawrence. "The womb in me roused to reach out to take him." There was not quite the same surge of blood on Lawrence's side. Lawrence says of Mabel, "Another 'culture-carrier,' likes to play the patroness, hates the white world and loves the Indian out of hate."

But he took to New Mexico itself. "The moment I saw the brilliant, proud morning shine high up over the deserts of Santa Fe," Lawrence wrote of the physical ambience, "something stood still in my soul, and I started to attend. There was a certain magnificence in the high-up day, a certain eagle-like royalty. . . . In the lovely morning of Australia one went into a dream. In the magnificent fierce morning of New Mexico one sprang awake, a new part of the soul woke up suddenly and the old world gave way to a new."

With Tony Luhan, Lawrence drove a long distance to an Apache feast at the Jicarilla reservation down in Lincoln County, scene of famous land wars only some

·

forty or fifty years before. He seems to have approved and then disapproved of what he observed. "The voice out of the far-off time was not for my ears. Its language was unknown to me. And I did not wish to know. . . . Our darkest tissues are twisted in this old tribal experience, our warmest blood came out of the old tribal fire. But they vibrate still in answer, our blood, our tissue. But me, the conscious me, I have gone a long road since then."

He wrote to E. M. Forster that, "I haven't got the hang of them [the Indians] yet." He was repelled by Mabel's electioneering over the Bursum Bill: "It has been the Bursum Bill till we're sick of it;" he still felt certain enough to write in the *New York Times* a paternalistic plea to white America: "Let us have the grace and dignity to shelter these ancient centers of life, so that, if die they must, they die a natural death."

Mabel Dodge Luhan, in love with her Indian and living in Taos in that fine pueblo-style house which still stands at the end of a laneway called Morada, wanted Lawrence to see it differently, wanted "to give him the truth about America: the false, new, external America in the east, and the true, primordial, undiscovered America that was preserved, living, in the Indian bloodstream."

But when Lawrence and Mabel began work together in her bedroom on a book on that theme, not only did she find a difference of ideology, but Frieda acted up as well.

"We can't go back," wrote Lawrence, opposing Mabel on the Indian question. "We cannot go back to the savages: not a stride. We can be in sympathy with them. We can take a great curve in their direction, onwards. But we cannot turn the current of our life backwards,

•

back towards their soft warm twilight and uncreate mud. . . . If we do it for a moment it makes us sick. We can only do it when we are renegade. . . . So many 're-formers' and 'idealists' who glorify the savages in America. They are death-birds, life-haters. Renegades."

Lawrence and Frieda spent the winter of 1922–23 at the Del Monte Ranch, north of Taos, in an abandoned ranch house in beautiful mountainous country covered with piñon pines. I was sad to find on the winter's day I went there that the road was closed off by a gate with a no-trespassing sign. But even now the whole feeling of the place is of remoteness. It makes you think of Law-rence as an adventurer; even though he was driven up here in part by fear of too much contact with "the un-speakable Mabel."

The unspeakable Mabel herself, in her house at the foot of the Sangre de Cristo mountains, would write her own mordant account of her association with Lawrence— *Lorenzo in Taos.* She would also ultimately publish her *Intimate Memories.* But as well, she could write lovingly, rhapsodically, hypnotically about New Mexico, in a way which shows none of the acquisitiveness she displayed toward Lawrence and which made Georgia O'Keeffe sus-picious of her and uncomfortable in her company.

Mabel writes of a Taos winter: "We have to follow the trail home through the snow that has covered it; we move through the bushes and trees that are suddenly white and bent under the swift and silent pressure, and we leave it to the horses to find the way. We reach our house before we expect it; it looms up all of a sudden, and if it is late afternoon, there will be a lighted window shining yellow. When we shake off the snow and go into the house, there is a warm smell from the narcissus and hyacinths that bloom all winter there. . . . But not more lovely than the cold, odorless world of ice and snow, where the piñons, cedar and sage are pungent with the magical oils they draw from the deep, living earth."

At the end of their winter, a winter such as our party of three found gives off a biting breath on the slopes of the Del Monte Ranch, the Lawrences expressed a passion to see old Mexico. They packed up and—for the moment—abandoned the literary and artistic enclaves of northern New Mexico.

Even on his second visit, Lawrence went on worrying about the Indian question. "You can perform the mental trick, and fool yourself and others into believing that the befeathered and bedaubed darling is nearer to the true ideal gods than we are. This last is just bunk, and a lie."

Mabel disapproved of something he wrote about a Hopi snake dance: "He had written a dreary *terre a terre* account of the long road to the Hopi village and of the dance, a mere realistic recital which might have been done by a tired, disgruntled businessman. It had no vision, no insight, no appreciation of any kind."

But Lawrence was an unrepentent Caucasian: "We dam the Nile and take the railway across America. The Hopi smooths the rattle snake and carries him in his mouth, to send him back into the dark places of the earth, an emissary to the inner powers."

Of course the Lawrence–Luhan debate is the crucial debate in our relationship to tribal people and is still being argued in New Mexico and elsewhere. For it does not seem to be sufficient for us to say: We are we, and they are they. We are driven somehow to work out a cultural batting order, and we rarely do it without excess in one direction or another.

•

Mabel deeded to Frieda the Flying Heart Ranch, again amongst the piñon pines north of Taos. Frieda would stay there till her death in 1959. Lawrence would make no further visits to New Mexico, for death was already thundering down upon him.

The consideration offered to Mabel in return for the Flying Heart Ranch was the manuscript of *Sons and Lovers*, today worth unutterable amounts. Mabel would ultimately sell it to pay her psychiatry bills.

IT WAS just before Lawrence's death that that great and simple eye of Georgia O'Keeffe came to New Mexico. She hoped to recover from a disastrous one-woman show in New York and from her painful association with the aging artist and photographer Alfred Stieglitz. She too was a guest at Mabel Dodge Luhan's house, but being a tolerant young woman, she was able to bear Mabel's fits of possessiveness. Georgia visited the Lawrence ranch but at a time the Lawrences were traveling in Europe, Lawrence himself sickening toward his end. Nonetheless she used the journey out there to the Arroyo Hondo area to paint her renowned 1929 painting, *The Lawrence Tree*.

She would express herself with a straightforward eloquence. "The world is wide here," she said of New Mexico, "and it's very hard to feel that it's wide in the East." Much of her New Mexico painting was a demonstration of this unadorned aphorism of hers. She was the New Mexican painter *par excellence*.

If you go looking for her type of painting around the plazas and in their neighboring streets these days, either in Santa Fe or in Taos, you will find many flashy but tawdry paintings. Ornamental renderings of various Indian events and costumes are common: The sort of paintings which are, in fact, in their sentimentality, the last stroke of the saber of the heavy cavalry of European culture. You *do* see, however, some paintings as clear-cut as O'Keeffe's, dealing in light and how it plays through windows and across the corners of adobe houses. And you see paintings which echo other O'Keeffe concerns; for example, paintings to do with the crosses of the Penitentes and the plain and glorious components of the New Mexico landscape.

YOU NEED a long time in Taos and Santa Fe to visit comprehensively the pueblos of the Pueblo.

The nearest to Santa Fe is Tesuque, which resembles a reservation anywhere in western America—prefabs and motor homes and a bingo hall, the bingo hall always a sign that "progressive" factions control the community. The more traditional San Ildefonso (named after the patron saint of farmers) stands in a bowl of dust near the east bank of the great river but has a perpetually clean-swept look and, like many pueblos, a classic adobe church. Ildefonso is the home of the wonderful maker of black pots, Maria Martínez, so admired by Georgia O'Keeffe. San Ildefonso goes in for separate adobe dwellings. It does not have the beehive look of the Hopi mesas and of Taos.

Further north, San Juan is the center for the Eight Northern Indian Pueblos Council, a body which represents Nambe pueblo, Picuris, San Ildefonso, San Juan, Santa Clara, Taos, Tesuque, and finally Pojoaque, which sits at the crossroads to Chimayo and atomic Los Alamos. Within each pueblo are a number of—generally—annually elected officials whose mandate derives from the time of Spanish occupation. The chief is *adalentado*, or governor. Two sub-*adalentados*, an *alguacil*, or police chief, and *fiscales*, parish authorities, form a sort of cabinet. With the office of *adelantado* comes two canes, and in most of the pueblos, there are three such canes available for use—the centuries-old ones the Spanish gave, the fancy silver-ferruled ones Abe Lincoln sent to each pueblo in 1863, and a third cherrywood and bronze one given by the government of New Mexico.

THE MOST renowned of all the pueblos is Taos.
Taos is built on a remarkable site at the foot of the Sangre de Cristo Mountains. Perhaps one should say *right at the foot*. The mountains are so close. The pueblo has been here at least since the Pueblo ancestors abandoned the Mesa Verde, Montezuma Valley, Hovenweep, and other areas—that is—since about 1300. The pueblo is largely made up of two apartment complexes lying north and south of a stream, Red Willow Creek, or Rio Pueblo. The stream comes roaring down in spring out of Blue Lake, which is itself fed by thirteen thousand feet-high Wheeler Peak's snowmelt. Taos Indians are very careful about the purity of this water: For seven centuries their health has depended on it.

The apartment structures rise to five stories, and there are watchtowers and five or six kivas separate from the complex.

The pueblo sits in its spring mud challenging our Eurocentric cast of thought as few places anywhere in

•

the United States do. It is in itself a statement of the contingency, the accidental nature of *our* remarkable, dazzling but relative culture. Just in its sweet appositeness, it requires that we adjust our minds to take in a broader image of humankind.

It draws you to ask what it must be like to live in such a beehive, where people are not close merely in living terms but also in terms of shared ritual and theology. There is some claustrophobic feeling to the pueblo of Taos. I read somewhere that the main form of social control here, the punishment for adultery, folly, theft, is laughter, mockery, and ridicule. Chuck Bowden, the Arizonan admirer of the Papago, says that this aspect of pueblo life terrifies him. He would rather be a more mobile desert nomad, despite all the hardships of that life. For movement and distance between clans would loosen those terrible instruments of tyranny which are so easy to wield amongst the cheek-to-cheek Pueblo: the aforesaid laughter and ridicule.

SOME WAY south of the fancy Santa Fe region of New Mexico, near the atomic capital of America, Alamagordo, we came to a surreal stretch of extraordinary pure white gypsum sand dunes, White Sands. Behind us (that is, to the east) were the Sacramento Mountains, gypsum themselves but looking benign enough with their wooded slopes and their snowcaps. Ahead (to the west) were the San Andres, similarly peaks of gypsum. And running for miles between, the unearthly white dunes.

This desolation is the Tularosa Basin, and even the

.

roads here are of pure white gypsum, fringed by white-out dunes. The dunes are held together by the occasional sanity-saving reference point of fourwing saltbush, a low shrub just like sagebrush.

We were told by a ranger how it all happened this way. Water from the mountains flowed down into Lake Lusero, the bottom of the Tularosa Basin, bringing gypsum flakes with it. The lake dried and still dries every summer, and the gypsum flakes are blown into dunes on the hot southwest wind.

Even in this abominable stretch—it is south of the Jornado del Muerto—futuristic New Mexico is represented: the White Sands Space Harbor lies nearby. The White Sands Missile Range to the south.

North of this bone-white memento mori, or this memento to be wary anyhow, lies the Trinity Test Site, where near the town of Oscuro (Dark), the biggest memento mori of the lot was touched off in 1945. This detonation made the whole world citizens of New Mexico. It was that final tasting of the tree of the knowledge of good and evil which has made us, alone amongst all species, godless. And stuck with our own mercy.

Trinity Site and White Sands are however quite a long way from where the bomb was developed. That happened up north again—and I ask the lenient reader to put up with another northward lunge. The atom bomb was made on the mesas of Los Alamos near Santa Fe. The globular bomb called Little Boy—an even cutesier and more offensive piece of nomenclature than Dinosaur Monument's Swelter Shelter—was then driven down here to Oscuro by way of Albuquerque, through sleeping towns—Los Lunas, Bernardo, San Acacia, Polvadera, Lemitar, Escondida, Socorro, San Antonio, Bingham,

•

THE PLACE WHERE SOULS ARE BORN

Carrizozo—on the night of Friday, July 13, 1945. As we all know, it worked impeccably.

Robert Oppenheimer, the atomic scientist, had in his childhood attended the Los Alamos Ranch School for Boys, and at his recommendation, it was acquired by Secretary of War Stimson in 1942 to be the isolated research base in which the bomb would be developed.

There is an enormous establishment up there now on the mesas northwest of Santa Fe: the Los Alamos National Laboratory. It employs so many people from the Santa Fe and Taos area that every day there is a traffic jam, morning and evening, on the precipitous New Mexico 502 which meets the main northern highway at the pueblo of Pojoaque. A National Laboratory museum called the Bradbury features not only models of Little Boy and Fat Man, but also an engrossing exhibit about the tensions between the scientists and their masters, particularly between Oppenheimer and General Leslie R. Groves, the soldier who had overall command of Los Alamos on behalf of the President.

In the enclave at Los Alamos lived an astounding collection of scientific talent. This is country not unlike Mesa Verde. It is made for isolation, each finger mesa open to intrusion only at one end. What had served the cliff dwellers of the twelfth century now served the scientists of the twentieth, and the scientists worked in the spirit of the geography. There was great intensity and an atmosphere of claustrophobic security. The Soviet spy Harry Gold *was* in the area—he communicated with the atomic physicist Klaus Emil Fuchs, met with him in Santa Fe, and went riding with him in the countryside. In Albuquerque too he made visits, which would later become famous, to an enlisted man from Los Alamos called

•

David Greenglass. Whenever Greenglass was in Albuquerque on leave and spending time with his wife, Gold turned up. Greenglass was the brother of Ethel Rosenberg of New York, who along with her husband, Julius, were idealistic Soviet spies who wanted to keep the world in balance by getting details of the bomb to the Soviets and who would later die in the electric chair for the treason of putting Gold in contact with their technologically adept nephew.

In Santa Fe and Albuquerque and elsewhere, in a countryside of Pueblo and cowboys and Hispanic bean farmers, a landscape only half-a-century secured from the Apache, Fuchs the scientist and Greenglass the intelligent enlisted man would pass to Gold a mass of documents and drawings which made the Soviet Union something close to full but secret partners in the Los Alamos technology. Documents, that is, which diagramed Armageddon. Greenglass for example handed Gold some perfect drawings and text concerning the *lens* of the bomb, the explosive device which would be used to focus detonations. Hence, through Gold, Fuchs, and Greenglass, the Soviets too became in their way citizens of New Mexico.

Three years later, Greenglass's unwillingness to escape from New York via Mexico on a Soviet spy underground to Scandinavia led to the arrest of all parties and the executions of the Rosenbergs.

WHILE GEORGIA O'Keeffe was building her house up in Abiquiu in 1944, the most astounding Promethean events were occuring nearby, on the finger mesas of Los Alamos.

·

THE PLACE WHERE SOULS ARE BORN

The building of the atomic bomb, pursued passionately in the furious atmosphere of World War II and in the monasterylike air of Los Alamos, often proceeded on a very primitive basis. And not only at Los Alamos. One is astounded to read in William Manchester's *The Glory and the Dream* that when the first nuclear pile at the University of Chicago had been built, people were uneasy about the limits of a chain reaction once started, about its capacity to run throughout the whole of Chicago or the whole of the United States or the whole of the universe. Young scientist-volunteers agreed to mount scaffolding above the pile. In case the cadmium and the boron already there failed to consume enough neutrons, they were to pour buckets of cadmium solution down into the catastrophe.

In Los Alamos itself the dangers seemed barely contained. In the dormitory sections, the cries of many justifiable nightmares were regularly heard.

There may be statues of Oppenheimer and General Groves in the museum at Los Alamos, but there isn't one to the nuclear martyr, Harry Dagnian. He was the first to know what others of us would find out in Hiroshima and Chernobyl. He was a young-to-youngish technician who was moving some fissionable material in Professor O. R. Frisch's laboratory one day when a chain reaction was set off. Radiation was released for just an instant. In the medical bay the nuclear physicians had their first chance to observe a human dying of severe radiation sickness. Gamma rays had affected all of Dagnian's vital organs. He died relatively quickly but, according to accounts, in great agony.

The most remarkable and Promethean nuclear cowboy was a young Canadian scientist named Lou Slotin,

•

who had flown a Spitfire in the RAF, had been grounded for some eye defect, and now came to Los Alamos to mess around with nuclear fire. I looked for some memorial plaque to him too, as to Dagnian, in the area of the Los Alamos nuclear laboratory which is open to the public. Once again, there is not one to be found.

The explosion in the proposed bomb was meant to occur when two live hemispheres of uranium, moving against each other, created a critical mass and produced the chain reaction. In the laboratory of Dr. Frisch, the one in which Dagnian had suffered his accident, Lou Slotin would frequently slide two hemispheres toward each other along a rod, impelling them forward with screw drivers. By all accounts, he played this game compulsively and against the advice of nearly everyone else in Los Alamos.

When an accident happened at last and the two hemispheres came too close to each other, there was a flash of blue light. Slotin had before him on the table a chain reaction capable of blowing up at least Los Alamos and thereby, of course, negating the government support the project had come to have up to that point. He tore the two hemispheres apart with his hands, even though that meant he received a fatal dose of radiation. Like Dagnian, he died a lonely radioactive death in the sick bay at Los Alamos.

SO IN that desolate basin called the Jornada del Muerto west of Oscuro, where Oñate's Spaniards had come close to death by thirst and where the Apache killed his son, one of Grove's three bombs—the one transported all the way from Los Alamos, consisting of two hemispheres of U235, a tamper, and a detonator—was set off on July 16, 1945, early in the morning, in a season of thunderstorms which, like Slotin's fiddling with screwdrivers, could have caused a premature explosion.

That spot in New Mexico was the first place on earth to experience, at least in human times, a temperature greater than that of the heart of the sun. People in Torrance, Lincoln, and Otaro Counties, like people in West Texas, felt the fierce nuclear wind blowing at their windows. The bombs waiting to be dropped on the enemy might have been called cute names, but Oppenheimer gave the event its true weight by quoting and making famous two passages from the Bhagavad Gita. "If the radiance of a thousand suns were to burst into the sky, that would be the splendor of the Mighty One!" And, "I am become Death, the shatterer of Worlds."

BENEATH THE atomic escarpments of Los Alamos lie the poor, sun-blasted and dust-ridden towns of rural and Hispanic New Mexico. Beneath the atomic cliffs lie the adobe churches—a particularly fine one at Chimayo; another dedicated to St. Francis, founder of the Franciscans, at Ranchos de Taos. And in the churches and houses and for sale on market days: the proliferation of hand-carved *santos* (saints), *bultos* (a bludgeonlike cross), *Guadalupes* (statues of the Virgin), and *Cristos*. New Mexico goes to the future in a state of ancient fervor.

Archbishop Lamy, as if to show that the Mexican excesses of Padre Martínez were not going to prevail against the authority of Rome, built a reddish, Romanesque, sandstone cathedral, one block from the Santa Fe Plaza. Lamy's fictional equivalent in Willa Cather's novel calls it "Midi Romanesque." "How exactly," writes Cather, "young Molny, his French architect, had done what he wanted! Nothing sensational, simply honest building and good stone-cutting, good Midi Romanesque of the plainest. And even now, in winter, when the acacia trees before the door were bare, how it was of the South, that church, how it sounded the note of the South!"

The "South" Latour/Lamy was trying to produce, of course, was the south of France. And the church itself is—in a way adobe isn't—a little severe and straightlaced, to match Lamy's Gallican, puritan spirit.

But there *is* an excessive and highly colored Mexican-style chapel off to one side of the cathedral. This is the chapel of the Conquistadora. The Conquistadora statue stands at the apogee of the altar panels. It is a minute, dolllike, and highly decorated Guadalupe, a Virgin Triumphant, dressed in satin and covered with donated ornaments. She is America's oldest Madonna. She came to Santa Fe at the beginning of the seventeenth century, was taken away by fleeing Spaniards when the Pueblo revolt began in 1680, and was brought back twelve years later, swaying in her own wagon, by Don Diego de Vargas. Since then she has been the center of a yearly festival and is the tutelary deity of the city.

French piety if not pietism sits next door to the cathedral in the Loretto Convent. This convent was originally staffed by good French nuns Lamy recruited. In the chapel (which is now a wing of a hotel chain franchise) stands a remarkable spiral staircase. It was built for the nuns by a mysterious carpenter in 1878. After the nuns

•

had made a novena to St. Joseph the carpenter, praying for an artisan capable of connecting the floor to the choir loft, a nameless, foreign tradesman blew into Santa Fe and produced without hammering a single nail an exquisite flight of stairs all of notched timber and lacking entirely in a central support pole.

It must have seemed an extraordinary piece of craftmanship to the nuns in Santa Fe, where everything was plain adobe and not always paintakingly constructed. And now in nuclear New Mexico, it is billed as a miracle. Since French and Mexican piety often intersect, you will find New Mexicans who will tell you as historic fact, the same sort of historic fact by which Lou Slotin died when the hemispheres got too close, that St. Joseph himself came up the Santa Fe trail and built the staircase at Loreto.

YOU WOULDN'T have read this book this far and been so patient if you did not expect a last reference to the Pueblo, the descendants of the Anasazi. In Taos pueblo one Friday afternoon, I saw eight men line up, each wearing the sort of headband which characterizes both the Pueblo and the Navajo Indians, a number wearing also a solitary feather, and all wearing aprons which had some lodge significance I did not understand. Some of them carried drums, the manufacture of which is one of Taos' crafts. These men began to march drumming and singing back and forth by the stream, the Rio Pueblo, which cuts the village in two. They were singing in a language called Tiwa or Tigua, which is spoken by a number of the northern Pueblo.

The differences of language amongst the Pueblo are significant. A related language, Tewa, is spoken by the more architecturally diffuse pueblos close to Santa Fe: San Ildefonso, Tesuque, Nambe, Santa Clara. The Jemez people from south of Los Alamos speak Towa, another dialect, or subgroup, of the overall language of all three groups, Tanoan. But then the Acoma, Zia, Santo Domingo, and Cochiti Pueblo speak a language entirely unconnected to Tanoan. It is called Keresan. Acoma people boast that no scholar is able to work out where it comes from. And on top of that, at Zuni, there is Zunian, which may have traveled up from Mexico centuries ago.

The singers and marchers of Taos anyhow were singing in Tiwa that Friday afternoon and practicing for a winter corn ceremony, since in the kivas at that stage of late winter, just as up at Walpi on the Hopi mesas, the corn and beans were beginning to sprout.

These ceremonies, with small differences, occur westward with the Zuni people as well; those great jewelers who come into Gallup to pawn their wares at the shops there, making of Gallup one big liquor store and pawn shop. Here at Taos, as at Zuni and elsewhere, the songs and marches and drummings were reviving the year and the world. To use an Australian aboriginal term, the lodge members of Taos were "singing up the country," making it safe from a complex of curses, including the curses unleashed at Los Alamos. There are the corn dances, the eagle dance, the basket dance, the snowbird, bow and arrow, feather, butterfly, turtle, horse, crow, basket, hoop, sun, cloud, Comanche, Kiowa, Navajo, dog, pine, evergreen dances; the snake dance which D. H. Lawrence found a limited stunt.

In the underworld of these Taos Pueblo Indians who

were practicing their late winter ceremony in the brisk air, it was not late winter at all but late summer, and the kachina deities were marching and dancing there in the true, subterranean earth; a march and a dance which paralleled the surface-of-the-earth dances of Picuris and Nambe, San Ildefonso and San Juan, Taos and Tesuque.

And in the Pueblo scheme, everything in the upper world has its equivalent spirit in the nether world. There is a kachina of Jim Beam whiskey. There is a kachina of the bomb. The dance redeems all, elevates all, restores all, neutralizes all.

Our journey through four of America's more startling provinces ends here, with these marching, singing Pueblo restoring the season. Of course there was still a fascinating road to be taken, and we took it. Up through Questa and Costilla, between huge mountains and into Colorado. Off then to Fort Garland and through La Veta Pass to Walsenburg. Past the superb mountains around Blanca Peak. Out of our responsibility to this record and for our own delight, we went to Aspen one last time, by way of Ute Pass and then tried Independence Pass, the latter closed in winter, even in this so-called mild or *Greenhouse* winter. So, we went the long way, through Glenwood Springs, the great spa town of the mining era. Knowing we were returning to Australia soon, we skied up the exquisite valley of Ashcroft, a mining town bypassed by the railway which came to Denver. From Ashcroft you can ski all the way to Crested Butte, and one day, after this book is written, we will do it.

We took a nostalgic journey down the so-called million dollar highway as well, the one cut through the mountains north of Durango—Louis L'Amour country— and then across to Gunnison, named for a soldier killed by the Ute, whose canyon is very strange, its walls black and vertical and utterly as sinister as say Zion, over in Utah.

But in the spirit of the book, it is the chanting we fix on, going away with it more or less in our ears. I take to the road strangely assured that someone is singing for us, celebrating matters we have got out of the way of celebrating for ourselves. The eternity of things. Even of our own spirits.

Acknowledgments

Amongst other works and documents on which this traveler drew, the following are notable: *Journey to the High Southwest*, Robert Casey; *The Southwest*, David Lavender; *Men to Match My Mountains*, Irving Stone; *Roadside History of Colorado*, James McTighe; *Utah: A People's History*, Dean L. May; *The Mormon Experience*, Leonard J. Arrington and Davis Bitton; *American Indians of the Southwest*, Bertha P. Dutton; *This is Dinosaur*, Wallace Stegner, ed.; *The Gathering of Zion: The Story of the Mormon Trail*, Wallace Stegner; *Desert Solitaire*, Edward Abbey; *The Journey Home*, Edward Abbey; *Killing the Hidden Waters*, Charles Bowden; *The Book of the Hopi*, Frank Waters; *Indian Running*, Peter Nabokov; *The Dancing Healers*, Carl A. Hammerschlag; *New Mexico*, Marc Simmons; *The Centuries of Santa Fe*, Paul Horgan; *Winter in Taos*, Mabel Dodge Luhan; *Portrait of an Artist: A Biography of Georgia O'Keeffe*, Laurie Lisle; *The Life of D. H. Lawrence*, Keith Sagar; *The Glory and the Dream*, William Manchester.

There are plenty of others too, some of them left on the road. I thank their authors and wish them renown.

In addition, such gracious people as Maxine Hong Kingston, Earl Kingston, Charles Bowden, and Bradley L. Patterson of Tucson steered me in the good directions. To them also, all the thanks and none of the blame.

•